the
ginger
survival guide

the ginger

survival guide

EVERYTHING THE REDHEAD NEEDS TO COPE
IN A CRUEL GINGERIST WORLD

TIM COLLINS

Michael O'Mara Books Limited

First published in Great Britain in 2006 by
Michael O'Mara Books Limited
9 Lion Yard
Tremadoc Road
London SW4 7NQ

A CIP catalogue record for this book is available from the British Library

ISBN (10-digit): 1-84317-184-8
ISBN (13-digit): 978-1-84317-184-3

3 5 7 9 10 8 6 4 2

www.mombooks.com

Design, typesetting and illustrations by Envy Design

Printed and bound in Slovenia by Printing House MKT print d.d. by arrangement
with Korotan, Ljubljana

contents

acknowledgements

Thanks to Mike Hughes, Collette Collins, Chris Maynard, Lindsay Davies, Judy Palmer, Alan Slater and Iain Millar, who spotted the need for this book in today's gingerist society. My thanks as well to all those ginners who shared their thoughts on coping with the condition.

introduction

It's Salem, Massachusetts, in the late seventeenth century, and a woman is being executed for witchcraft.

The evidence?

She has red hair.

Red hair, like Mary Magdalene.

Red hair, like Judas Iscariot.

Red hair, red like the very fires of Hell.

Jump forward 300 years and the persecution continues. Only instead of 'witch', the cry is now 'carrot top'. Instead of Satanism, the accusation is 'drinking too much Sunny D', and instead of Mary Magdalene and Judas, the association is with Geri Halliwell and Chris Evans.

Throughout history, gingers have been stigmatized, ostracized and punished. But now the time has come for redheads to fight back against their oppressors.

If you belong to the world's least-acknowledged minority group, *The Ginger Survival Guide* will give you all the information and advice you'll need to fight gingerphobia. You'll find out about the scientific causes of red hair, the historical struggle of the gingers, and the lives of those coppertops who've truly made a difference to the world around them. You'll also get tips on how to survive in today's intolerant gingerist society – tips that will transform even the most apologetic 'strawberry blonde' into a ginger ninja.

This book heralds a momentous time – the time for ginners to rise up and proclaim with one unified voice:

'Yes! We have ginger hair. Yes! We have freckles. And yes, we have bright orange pubes. *But we are not ashamed.'*

11

how ginger are you?

Let's begin by finding out what kind of ginge you are. You'll read more about the pigment called melanin in the next chapter, but suffice it to say at this point that because the amount of 'light' melanin in hair varies from person to person, a spectrum of gingerness exists that encompasses the almost-blonde to the almost-brown. If you have a faint suspicion that you may be a carrot top, place a lock of your hair against the handy colour chart below to determine your official ginger rating.

BLONDE	If you're blonde and you've picked up this book then you probably did so by mistake. In fact, if you're blonde and you've picked up any book you probably did so by mistake.
STRAWBERRY BLONDE	The term 'strawberry blonde' is often used by ginger traitors seeking to brand themselves as in some way blonde. Like that's such a good thing. But you genuinely are a strawberry blonde – fair-haired but with a ginger tint.
GOLDEN BLONDE	Your hair lies halfway between strawberry blonde and total ginner. You probably called yourself 'strawberry blonde' to avoid childhood teasing, but call yourself a 'redhead' now – it's more fashionable.

PROPER GINGER	None of this wishy-washy strawberry-blonde nonsense for you. You're a proper carrot who looks like their head has been painted by Stelios. Better still, you've probably got pale skin, light eyes and a smattering of freckles too. Marvellous stuff. Be proud.
AUBURN GINGER	Your hair is slightly darker than the full-on carrot top, but you're still distinctively ginge. Like 'strawberry blonde', the term 'auburn' is sometimes used as a euphemism for 'ginger', as when hair-dye manufacturers divide their ginger product range into 'light', 'medium' and 'dark auburn'.
COPPER GINGER	Now we're moving towards the brunette end of the ginger spectrum. At some point in your life you've probably been called 'coppertop' or 'Duracell', and been accused of standing in the rain for so long that your hair went rusty.
BRUNETTE	Sorry, but you're not even a little bit ginger. I know you'd like to gain some minority-group street cred, but you're barking up the wrong tree with this whole ginger thing. Have you thought about becoming a gay?

RED GINGER

Hmm. Although we often use the word 'red' to describe hair, it doesn't naturally grow this colour. Which means you're a shameless ginger wannabe who knows nothing of the true struggle of the genuine ginge. Hang your head.

ginger faq

Do all gingers have pale skin?

Despite all the jokes you've heard about getting sunburn from light bulbs, the red-hair gene is not exclusive to light-skinned people. In fact, there's a small population of redheads in Jamaica, who are surely the only people in the world who can carry off the 'ginger dreadlocks' hairstyle.

RED CORNER

'Redheaded women are either violent or false, and usually are both.'

French proverb

So where exactly does ginger hair come from? If you want to combat gingerphobia, you need to find out the real origins of red hair.

It's time for a quick science lesson. Ginger hair is basically caused by a pigment called melanin. There are two types of this pigment: 'light' melanin and 'dark' melanin. Any one person has both types in their hair. If you have a high level of dark pigment and a low level of light pigment, you'll have dark hair. On the other hand, if you have a low level of dark pigment and a high level of light pigment, you'll have blonde or ginger hair. Because the relative amount of pigment is different in everyone, it creates a complex spectrum of gingerness (as seen in the previous chapter).

Gingers tend to have fewer hairs on their heads than other people, averaging just 90,000, compared to 110,000 for brunettes and 140,000 for blondes. So it's official – blondes really are thicker.

The ginger gene

The ginger gene – the Melanocortin-1 receptor gene – was only discovered in 1997. Yes, the sad truth is that mankind invented the spork and the electric ear- and nose-hair trimmer before it got around to explaining gingerness.

The Melanocortin-1 receptor gene is recessive, which means that you must inherit it from both parents to be a ginge. The brown-hair gene is dominant, so if you inherit one ginger gene and one brown-hair gene brown hair will win. However, you could still carry the ginger gene and have a ginger child if your partner carries it too.

This leads to instances where two non-gingers who both carry the gene give birth to a ginger child, which inspires the inevitable jokes about the milkman (see 'The Milkman Joke', page 58).

Unfortunately, some scientists believe that the recessive ginger gene could die out as early as one hundred years from now. Unless, that is, everyone agrees to have as much sex as possible with ginners, and thereby save the gene.

Well, it's worth a try.

Gingers and natural selection

So what exactly is the point of gingas? According to Darwin's theory of evolution by natural selection, an organism's (or in this case, a ginner's) traits, should they turn out to be advantageous to survival, will be passed down to future generations. So, given that there are gingers in the world, what advantage does ginger hair offer?

The truth is, nobody really knows. You'd think that bright red hair would have made it harder for gingers to hide from predators, and that the gene would have died out long ago. But maybe all the predators had heard about how hard gingers were and decided to steer clear.

Perhaps the most flattering way of explaining the survival of the gene is

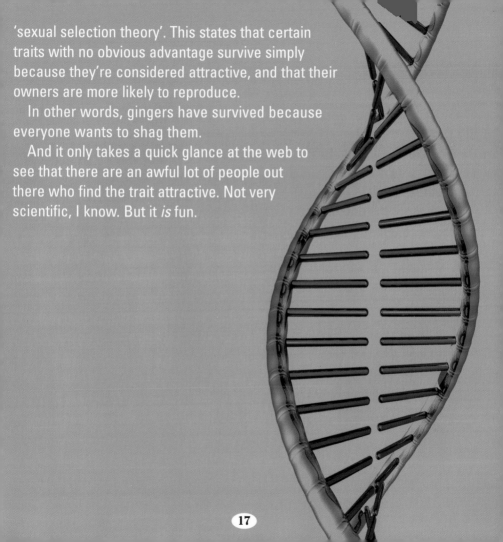

'sexual selection theory'. This states that certain traits with no obvious advantage survive simply because they're considered attractive, and that their owners are more likely to reproduce.

In other words, gingers have survived because everyone wants to shag them.

And it only takes a quick glance at the web to see that there are an awful lot of people out there who find the trait attractive. Not very scientific, I know. But it *is* fun.

the ginger hall of fame:
great gingers in history

Many gingers take pride in knowing how many great men and women over the years have been rusty-follicled. But how much do you know about your heritage, and about those who have blazed a fiery trail before you?

Don't worry if you need to swot up. The Ginger Hall of Fame is on hand to celebrate the lives of those who've made the world a gingerer place.

Throughout history, redheads have made a remarkable contribution to world events. They've been kings, queens, explorers, writers, artists and scientists. Here are some of the greats the world would never have seen if it hadn't been for the Melanocortin-1 receptor.

Napoleon Bonaparte (1769–1821)

Ginger emperor of France who, in the late eighteenth and early nineteenth centuries, started on virtually every other European country. According to popular belief, Bonaparte did this because he was suffering from 'short-man syndrome' and subconsciously sought to compensate for his lack of height. However, Napoleon was in fact almost 5 feet 7 inches tall, which was above average for a Frenchman back then. It's far more likely that he got teased about being a ginge and that's what set him off.

Boudicca (d. AD 62)

Redheaded British queen who led her people, the Iceni, against the occupying Roman forces in the first century AD. Had a spat with fellow ginner Nero, which resulted in the pillaging of Roman settlements and the almost total destruction of London. Just goes to show what can happen when gingers fight among themselves.

Winston Churchill (1874–1965)

Although most of it was gone by the time he became Prime Minister in 1940, Sir Winston's hair was originally curly and ginger. This will have won him few favours with arch-nemesis Hitler, who was more attracted to muscular blokes with blonde hair and blue eyes, according to Channel 5 documentaries.

Christopher Columbus (1451–1506)

Flame-haired Italian-born explorer who discovered America in 1492. So not only was he a top ginner, but without him we wouldn't have American ginger icons such as Molly Ringwald, Garfield and Fanta. And what kind of a world would that be?

Emily Dickinson (1830–1886)

Red-haired American poet who was virtually unknown in her lifetime, but has subsequently become recognized as one of the greatest poets of the nineteenth century. In contrast to the ginger stereotype of being outgoing and vivacious, Dickinson didn't meet anyone who was not a member of her immediate family until she was in her thirties. Perhaps she was embarrassed by her colouration. We'll never know.

Henry VIII (1491–1547)

Ginger king whose scandalous womanizing shocked England, making him the Mick Hucknall of his day. Except that instead of treating the ladies to sophisticated, middle-of-the-road soul pop, he beheaded them. Which doesn't sound too bad when you put it like that.

Galileo Galilei (1564–1642)

Ginger Italian physicist, astronomer and small-scale inventor whose achievements include pioneering experimental science, discovering the first and second laws of motion and getting told off by the Catholic Church for suggesting that the earth moves around the sun. As an inventor he made vital improvements to the telescope, the thermometer and the microscope, although his sketchbooks show he also had some rubbish ideas such as a comb that could be used as a fork.

Florence Nightingale (1820–1910)

Redhead who revolutionized the British health-care system in the nineteenth century and along the way pioneered modern nursing. Remains to this day the greatest ginger nurse in history. And that includes Duffy from *Casualty*.

Mary Magdalene (1st century BC–1st century AD)

Although Mary's hair colour is not referred to in the Bible, portraits of her by Titian, Rossetti and Donatello show her as flame-haired. Given that ginger hair was typically associated with the supernatural, fans of *The Da Vinci Code* might view this as part of the conspiracy to demonize Magdalene and repress the sacred feminine. But it's just as likely that the artists in question were filthy old gingerphiles who preferred using red-haired models.

Titian (c.1488–1576)

It wasn't just Mary Magdalene that Titian depicted as a ginge. In fact, he painted so many gingers that he inspired a fashion for red hair among sixteenth-century women. Although given the scarcity of Clairol back then, they had to use mixtures of alum, sulphur, soda and rhubarb to achieve the look. The word 'Titian' is still used today to describe reddish-brown hair, and is probably a better description than 'coppertopped' if you're writing a personal ad.

James Joyce (1882–1941)

Ginger author of *Dubliners*, *A Portrait of the Artist as a Young Man*, *Ulysses* and *Finnegans Wake*. *Ulysses* is often cited as the greatest novel of the twentieth century, while *Finnegans Wake* is the most experimental work of fiction ever to have had some pubs named after it, unless there's a 'Mrs Dalloway and Firkin' somewhere I've missed.

a brief history of gingerism

Taunts of 'ginger minger' may be distressing, but ginger intolerance is not a recent phenomenon. In fact, ginners have been regarded with prejudice and fear throughout history. And some of the persecution they've met with has been even worse than having cans of Tizer poured over them in the school playground.

The ancient Egyptians, for example, believed that redheads were unlucky and are even thought to have burnt and buried them alive in an effort to eradicate them.

The ancient Greeks also feared ginners, believing that their 'humours' (the four fluids of the body thought in classical times to determine a person's personality) were in the wrong proportions, and that they turned into vampires when they died. Which, if true, would be good news for the ginger goth community.

The advent of Christianity didn't help the coppertop cause much either, as the colour red became associated with Satan and the fires of Hell. This inspired a fresh round of persecution, as when ginger hair was cited as evidence of witchcraft during the Spanish Inquisition. If a woman's hair was the colour of the Devil, they argued, it proved she was in league with him, and should be burnt. Sales of henna duly plummeted.

The belief that gingerness was supernatural survived for centuries, and is reflected in carrot-topped mythological creatures such as leprechauns and banshees. More recently, red-haired clown Ronald McDonald has demonstrated many supernatural powers, such as making burgers and fries appear from nowhere, magically transporting children to a branch of McDonald's, as well as making a giant yellow 'M' appear in the air just by tracing its shape with his fingers.

Many works of art also reflect the gingerist attitudes of their times. Some Renaissance works, for example, depict Judas with red hair, and this helped give credence to the belief that gingers are untrustworthy – a cruel misconception that survives to this day, even to the extent that it was voiced by Labour MP Frank Dobson in 2000 (see the 'Notorious Gingerphobes' chapter starting on page 51).

For a transparent example of gingerism at work, have a look at Michelangelo's fresco of *The Temptation* on the ceiling of the Sistine Chapel. Eve has brown hair when she takes the fruit from the serpent. But, after eating the fruit, losing her innocence and being expelled from the Garden of Eden, she's suddenly turned into a redhead. The hussy.

Gingerism has also tainted depictions of Eve's oldest son, Cain. The book of Genesis tells how Cain kills his brother Abel. To punish him, God makes Cain wander the earth, and places a mark on him. The Bible doesn't specify what this mark is, but some paintings have depicted it as red hair. The belief that gingerness was a curse from God was used to justify yet more coppertop persecution.

So the next time someone makes a 'hilarious' joke about ginger pubes, or gets you a bag of carrots for the office Secret Santa, at least be grateful that they aren't rounding up the locals, building a fire beneath you and burning you at the stake. You could have it much worse.

ginger faq

Why do some non-gingers have ginger beards?

Some blokes with blonde or dark hair start sprouting ginger facial hair when puberty hits. This is not because they've been hiding cans of Clairol under their beds since they were babies, but because they're carrying the ginger gene without actually having red hair. These hapless teens then have to choose between removing all trace of their facial hair and getting teased for looking young, or proudly displaying their bumfluff, and getting teased for being a semi-ginge. Life is cruel.

RED CORNER

'There was never a saint with red hair.'
Russian proverb

the ginger hall of shame:
ginger traitors

As well as celebrating the lives of inspirational ginners, *The Ginger Survival Guide* also exposes those who've brought shame to the redhead community.

This first Hall of Shame brings to light those who are guilty of perhaps the most heinous crime of all – dyeing their hair another colour. Even the gingerest gingers have been known to refer to their hair as 'strawberry blonde' at some point in their lives, but some treacherous individuals have taken their traitorous impulses even further.

Billie Joe Armstrong – Green Day
Green Day may pride themselves on being a bona fide punk band in a sea of pop-punk imitators. But look closely at the roots of singer Billie Joe Armstrong's 'black' hair and you'll see that not everything about them is authentic.

Tim Cully – *Big Brother 3*

The posh star of the third series of *Big Brother* caused a tabloid stir when it was revealed that he was secretly dyeing his ginger hair black. He then made things worse by even denying he was a ginner in the first place.

The ultimate ginger traitor, Cully is redeemed only by the fact that he had the decency to disappear without trace after the show, rather than landing a presenting job on a cable channel.

Goths

Take a close look at those moody teens drinking snakebite next to the local war memorial. The chances are you'll see a few ginger roots beneath all that black hair.

Given that red hair traditionally has supernatural associations, it seems strange that so many ginger goths choose to disguise their natural colour. Plus, you only need to look at Shirley Manson from Garbage to see that the red-haired goth look can work.

Still, joining the local goth gang isn't such a bad idea if you're a ginge. You've already got the pale skin, so you'll save a packet on foundation, and the chances of them inviting you on a sunbathing holiday in Ibiza are pretty slim.

OUTED

Marilyn Monroe

The world's most famous ditzy blonde was in fact a ditzy ginger by nature. If only she'd been true to herself, she might have been given more fulfilling redhead roles, thus avoiding becoming a tragic icon, and we'd have been spared that bloody Elton John song.

Ginger Rogers

Like Marilyn Monroe, Ginger Rogers dyed her red hair blonde to further her career as a young starlet. Unlike Monroe, however, her name was a bit of a giveaway, making her the least successful pigmentary traitor before Michael Jackson.

Malcolm X

He may be one of the most famous black activists in history, but Malcolm X's hair was originally ginger, and he was even nicknamed 'Detroit Red' in his youth. He spent his life combating racism, but the issue of gingerism was tellingly absent from his impassioned speeches.

George Washington

Although renowned for not being able to tell a lie, Washington actually powdered his ginger hair to make it seem whiter. This traitorous act aside, Washington did at least start a trend for ginger US presidents.

Thomas Jefferson, Martin Van Buren, Andrew Jackson, Ulysses S. Grant, Calvin Coolidge and Dwight Eisenhower all followed, adding up to an impressive total of seven redheads out of forty-three US presidents.

exposing ginger traitors

Do you suspect someone of being a closet ginger? Perhaps you thought you saw some ginger roots, but aren't quite sure. Maybe you've caught them tapping their feet to the raunchy sound of Simply Red? Encourage them to reveal their true ginner nature by exposing them with these simple traps:

- Tell them they've got something in their eye. Use this as an excuse to check for red eyelashes and freckles.

- Propose that everyone in the office brings in a childhood photo. Do they claim not to have one? Perhaps they're hiding something.

- Suggest popping down to the park for a spot of lunchtime sunbathing. Are they suddenly too busy? The evidence mounts.

- Use phrases like 'collar and cuffs' and 'fire down below' in conversation with them. Do they look uncomfortable?

- Find out if your victim covers up their freckles with foundation by making a surprise early morning visit to their house.

- Leave a high-factor suncream lying around and see if they can resist digging into it.

- Keep a close watch on their hands. See any mysterious stains? It could mean they've been at the hair dye.

- If your victim is the same sex as you, suggest popping down to the gym with them after work. Do they avoid the communal showers?

As soon as you've got enough evidence, confront your victim. Explain that gingerness is nothing to be ashamed of and demand that they end the hypocrisy. Let them know that if they don't tell everyone the truth about their true carrot-bonced nature, you will.

ginger faq

Can you really turn ginger from eating too many Wotsits?

No. But it is possible that you could turn ginger if you ate no food at all. A rare condition called kwashiorkor, which turns dark hair ginger, occurs in cases of extreme malnutrition. But despite what you may have heard, there's no evidence as yet linking the condition to Wotsits, Irn-Bru or Sunny Delight.

ginger insults

A staggeringly large number of abusive terms aimed at gingers have been devised over the years. Even worse, it's difficult to think of any specific insults at all for people with other hair colours.

This section contains some of the most offensively gingerphobic slurs ever coined. Some of you may find these expressions upsetting. But *The Ginger Survival Guide* believes that redheads should be prepared for the abusive language they might encounter, and should be aware of the appropriate comebacks.

However, it's vitally important that this section is kept out of reach of non-gingers, especially those with gingerist tendencies – they need no more ammunition than they already have.

RATINGS KEY:

1 = Inoffensive | **2** = Mildly upsetting | **3** = Unacceptable | **4** = Offensive | **5** = Hate crime

'Beaker'

An insult comparing the victim to the *Muppet Show* character. Works best if they have spiky red hair, a lab coat and a permanent expression of surprise. To devise a comeback, simply use the name of the *Muppet Show* character your tormentor most resembles. Do they have blonde hair and a snout? Are they small and green? Do they play the drums with their head?
Gingerist rating:

'Carrot top'
The most popular of all the gingerphobic insults, there can be few true gingers who've never been on the receiving end of this one. The correct comeback is, of course, 'Actually the top of a carrot is green, not orange.'
Gingerist rating: ////

'Casper'
As in 'the friendly ghost'. This is a reference to translucent skin rather than hair colour, and is therefore quite inventive. If you're called this name, you should point out that Casper never actually had ginger hair, and that the insult would be a better name for an albino. Although if you've got one of those in your neighbourhood, you've probably already nicknamed them 'The Milky Bar Kid'.
Gingerist rating: ///

'Coppertop' / 'copperknob' / 'ginger minge' / 'rusty gusset'
The first is a reasonably tame schoolyard insult. The others are spinoffs from it, and are examples of the many insults that work on the supposition that if someone has ginger hair on their head, then they also have it in their pubic region. As with any pubes-based insult the correct playground comeback is, of course, 'At least I've got some pubes.' This doesn't work quite so well when you're thirty-five.
Gingerist rating: ////

'Duracell'

One of the many ginger taunts that compare the victim to a product featuring the colours orange, red or copper. Reasonably imaginative, but only really accurate if your hair colour is somewhere between auburn and brown. And if you always dress entirely in black.

Gingerist rating: ///

'Freckle head' / 'freckle features'

Getting teased about your freckles at least makes a change from getting teased about your hair. The term 'freckle head' is largely inoffensive, unless it's combined with the notion that freckles are a contagious disease like chicken pox, the lurgy or cooties. If you're teased in this way the solution is obvious. Simply touch your tormentors and tell them that they've caught freckles off you.

Gingerist rating: ////

'Ginga' / 'ginner'

Modern variations of the word 'ginger', and pronounced with hard Gs. 'Ginga' seems to be especially popular at the time of writing, probably because it rhymes properly with 'minger'.

Gingerist rating: ///

'Ginger biscuit' / 'Ginger nut'

'Ginger biscuit' was a spectacularly uninventive insult used in infant school. 'Ginger nut' at least picked a specific type of biscuit and made a punning reference to the head, but is, frankly, still a bit lame.

Gingerist rating: /

'Ginger minger'

Given the similarity in the sound of these two slang terms, they were always going to end up together. Although redheads can take *some* comfort from the fact that the words don't quite rhyme as well as they should. It's appropriate to counter this insult by suggesting that your tormentor is even more minging. As in, 'What does that make you, then? Ming the Merciless?'

Gingerist rating: /////

'Ginger ninja'

Unusually, a ginger nickname that makes you sound pretty hard. Sadly, it's more likely to be the kind of nickname that you'd invent for yourself rather than one that others would give you.

Gingerist rating: /

'Ginger whinger'

Yet another rhyme-based insult, and also the nickname the tabloids gave to Neil Kinnock in the eighties and Chris Evans in the nineties. This is quite a difficult insult to disprove, as any attempt at protest will be cited as evidence of ginger whinging. It's best just to ignore this one if it's slung your way.

Gingerist rating: ////

'Little Orphan Annie'

Bog-standard association of ginger-haired person with ginger-haired fictional character. Could potentially become much more offensive if the ginger in question really is an orphan.

Gingerist rating: ///

'Period head'

Given that pointing at anything red and saying 'period' is a dead cert for a playground laugh, it's no surprise that the link between red hair and menstruation is frequently made. Obviously, if someone with brown hair says that your hair is the colour of period, the traditional comeback is to point out that theirs is the colour of poo. And if they are blonde, you point out that theirs is the colour of wee. Hardly Oscar Wilde, I know. But it does the job.

Gingerist rating: ////

'Ronald McDonald's love child'

A gingerist taunt that's made all the more unpleasant for evoking mental images of a scary clown having sex with your mum. As with any parental insults, the correct comeback is, 'At least I've got a dad.'

Gingerist rating: /////

'Satan's love child'

As we saw in the 'A Brief History of Gingerism' chapter, the link between Satan and red hair has been around for centuries, and even provoked the hanging of supposed witches. Taunts like 'Satan's love child' and 'Devil spawn' still survive in playgrounds today, although one hopes they won't be followed by ritual murder.

Gingerist rating: /////

'Sunny Delight'

A taunt that was especially popular in the mid-nineties amid alarmist tabloid reports that drinking Sunny Delight was turning children orange. Putting two and two together, many playground taunters concluded that any ginger pupils in their school must have drank so much Sunny D that it went straight to their hair. Counter-rumours initiated by a small ginger resistance movement that claimed brown-haired kids had been drinking too much Pepsi and blonde-haired kids had been drinking too much Lemon Fanta failed to catch on.

Gingerist rating: /////

the ginger hall of fame:
ginger cartoon characters

Many animators have dipped their brushes into the red paint over the
years, using a character's ginger hair to signify their fieriness,
rebelliousness or sexiness – all the best traits in our favourite ginners.
This section of the Ginger Hall of Fame salutes the two-
dimensional coppertops who've inspired us all.

Ariel – *The Little Mermaid*
Red-haired mermaid from the popular Disney cartoon.
In Chapter 61 of Dan Brown's *The Da Vinci Code*,
Robert Langdon claims that 'the Little Mermaid's
flowing red hair was certainly no coincidence', and
that the film is 'a ninety-minute collage of blatant
symbolic references to the lost sanctity of Isis, Eve,
Pisces the fish goddess and, repeatedly, Mary Magdalene'. Yes, Mr Brown.
Either that, or it's a cartoon about a mermaid and a singing crab.

Daredevil
In the Marvel comic *Daredevil*, blind (and ginger) attorney Matt Murdock
becomes one of the greatest superheroes of all time, despite his crippling
disability. The blindness, I mean. Not the gingerness.

Daphne Blake – *Scooby Doo*

Paranormal investigator who lives in a van with stoners and dogs. Much sexier than she sounds. In fact, she was such a flame-haired minx that Fred would often suggest the team should temporarily split up, palming frumpy brunette Velma off on Shaggy and Scooby while he and Daphne went off to 'investigate' alone.

Droopy

Lazy cartoon dog, created by Tex Avery in the 1940s, who had white fur on his body and ginger hair on his head. Droopy was known for his deadpan outsmarting of enemies, which made it all the more surprising when Droopy's son Dripple turned up in nineties spin-off *The Tom and Jerry Kids*. After all, the idea of Droopy frantically rutting a bitch was slightly at odds with his nonchalant, on-screen persona.

Wilma Flintstone – *The Flintstones*

Reasonably attractive ginger wife of Fred Flintstone. Not quite as fit as Daphne from *Scooby Doo*, nor Jane Jetson, but if she was up for it, Fred was away from home, and it was possible to have sex with a cartoon character, you probably would.

Fry – *Futurama*
The hero of Matt Groening's sci-fi comedy. Travelling to the year 3000, he transports the ginger gene to a time long after it would have otherwise died out. Unfortunately, Fry was such a flop with the ladies that a ginger revival was never really on the cards.

Groundskeeper Willie – *The Simpsons*
Irascible, yellow-skinned janitor from America's longest-running sitcom. Willie's red hair is one of his many stereotypical Scottish traits, which also include kilt wearing, whisky drinking, football hooliganism and hating the English.

George and Jane Jetson
Hanna-Barbera optimistically chose a red-haired couple for their futuristic *Flintstones* retread, ignoring the scientific theory that the recessive ginger gene would be all but gone by the late twenty-first century.

Garfield
Overweight ginger cat, often seen eating lasagne, sleeping on the TV chair and attached to the inside of car windows. As with Steve Davis, Garfield's laid-back, deadpan persona flies in the face of fiery redhead stereotypes.

Josie McCoy – *Josie and the Pussycats*

Redheaded, sexually charged lead singer of the fictional girl-group Josie and the Pussycats, who collectively, at various times since the sixties, have featured in a comic, a Hanna-Barbera animated series and a live-action movie. Unlike so many of today's safe rock stars like Keane and Coldplay, JATP weren't afraid to get caught up in an adventure on the way to a gig, possibly involving a mad scientist, a spy or an alien.

Poison Ivy – *Batman*

Ginger villainess and enemy of Batman, and played by Uma Thurman in 1997 film *Batman and Robin*. Poison Ivy plotted to destroy humanity and install in our place a race of plants, and was regarded as the world's sexiest ginger botanist before Charlie Dimmock came along.

Jessica Rabbit – *Who Framed Roger Rabbit?*

Roger Rabbit's trophy wife is reckoned to be the sexiest cartoon character ever created. She's presumably open to a spot of bestiality, though sadly the film stops short of depicting this.

gingerphilia

-philia
Denoting fondness, esp. an abnormal love for a specified thing

Gingerphilia
Denoting fondness, esp. an abnormal love for a ginner

Given that other documented paraphilias include attraction to asphyxiation, old people and furry animal costumes, gingerphiles really don't do too badly.

Some gingerphiles in the US call themselves 'redophiles', although if you choose to use this term you're only a simple mishearing away from an angry mob of *News of the World* readers turning up on your doorstep.

If you're worried that you might be a gingerphile yourself, check for the following telltale signs:

- Do you have a fetish for pale skin, freckles or ginger pubes?

- Do you consider Nicola Roberts to be the best-looking member of Girls Aloud?

- As a child, did you feel strange and confused when Daphne from *Scooby Doo* was on TV?

- Have you ever requested that your partner dress up as the Little Mermaid, Pippi Longstocking or Ronald McDonald?

- Have you ever been a sex tourist in Scotland?

- Did you only start to find Geri Halliwell annoying when she dyed her hair blonde?

If you answered 'yes' to any of the above questions, you may be a gingerphile. But don't panic. As the next section shows, many famous and successful people share your fetish.

ginger faq

Should I go out with another ginger?

Many gingers think it would feel a bit weird to have a relationship with a fellow coppertop. And it's certainly true that many people will assume you're brother and sister, which will make public snogging a problem. Unless you live in Norfolk.

But think about the advantages. Firstly, according to the stereotypes, you'll both be really good in bed. And secondly, if you have kids together, you'll be doing your bit to save the ginger gene.

noted gingerphiles

It's not just one-handed Internet surfers who suffer from scarlet fever. Here are a few self-confessed ginger lovers. Ladies, get to know their type. It could make your life as a redhead a lot easier.

Mark Antony

The Roman general was so taken with Cleopatra – who coloured her hair red using henna – that he moved to Alexandria to live with her. Blaise Pascal famously claimed that had Cleopatra's nose been shorter, the whole face of the world would have changed. But you only need to look at a portrait of the massive-conked mathematician to guess why he chose Cleopatra's long nose as an indication of her beauty. It's far more likely that her flowing red mane was the feature that snared Antony.

Charlie Brown

In *Peanuts*, the object of Charlie Brown's unrequited love was known simply as 'The Little Red-Haired Girl'. We never knew her name, we never saw her, and she remained tantalizingly out of reach for shy, prematurely bald gingerphile Charlie.

Fred Flintstone

Anyone who would choose mumsy redhead Wilma over her more

attractive dark-haired friend Betty Rubble has got to have a serious thing about gingas.

The Pre-Raphaelites

The nineteenth-century Pre-Raphaelite Brotherhood managed to make money out of pictures of naked redheads even before the Internet existed. Dante Gabriel Rossetti, one of the founders of the brotherhood, was such a gingerphile that he had a red-haired wife *and* a red-haired mistress.

Bruce Springsteen

Rock star who married the E Street Band's ginger guitarist Patti Scialfa. Springsteen wrote a gingerphile song called 'Red Headed Woman', in which he claims that red-haired women know how to get 'the dirty job done'. At the time of this book going to press, the world of rock has yet to produce a song about how good in bed ginger blokes are, but I'm sure it's on its way. Possibly.

Wallace – *Wallace and Gromit*

Wide-mouthed northerner made from plasticine. Wallace's obsession with orange cheese in the early animations hinted at gingerphile tendencies. These tendencies were made explicit when he fell in love with red-haired Wendolene in *A Close Shave*.

the ginger hall of fame:
ginger sex symbols

As any gingerphile will tell you, redheads are the most attractive people on the planet. This chart of ginger sex symbols therefore officially replaces those polls found in magazines like *FHM* and *Heat* as the definitive list of the world's most fanciable people.

Mick Hucknall – Simply Red

He may look like Charlie Drake, but that hasn't stopped Hucknall from becoming the world's top ginger male slag.

Cleopatra

This henna ginge was so beautiful she changed the entire course of history. She still doesn't beat Mick Hucknall, though.

Julianne Moore and Nicole Kidman

Debate often rages among gingerphile blokes about whether (given the choice) they'd shag Julianne Moore or Nicole Kidman. And I bet they'll be glad they gave the issue due consideration if they ever find themselves in a situation where Julianne and Nicole are fighting over them.

Jessica Rabbit

Ginger bombshell wife of Roger Rabbit. It's well known amongst gingerphiles that a quick snatch of Jessica's snatch was included in *Who Framed Roger Rabbit?* by disgruntled animators. Pause the scene where Jessica and Eddie are thrown out of the cab and advance it frame by frame to find out if she's a natural redhead.

Ariel – The Little Mermaid

Sexy mermaid with the bottom half of a fish and the top half of a woman. Would probably be less sexy if it was the other way round.

Patsy Palmer

Bianca from *EastEnders* might not be anybody's first choice in the seduction stakes, but she at least has that all-important attainability factor.

Julia Roberts

Probably wouldn't have got away with calling her breakthrough movie *Pretty Woman* if she'd looked like Lizzie Bardsley from *Wife Swap*.

Woody Allen

Allen might now look like a bald, frail old man, but in his films he always seems to end up with attractive young girls. Could be something to do with the fact that he writes and casts all his movies himself.

Rula Lenska

Polish actress who became a major sex symbol following the success of seventies drama *Rock Follies*. Lenska re-emerged on *Celebrity Big Brother* in 2006, and proved that she still had the raw sexual power to make respected MPs pretend to be cats and lick imaginary cream off their whiskers.

Anne Robinson

If mature, plastic matriarchs with red hair are your type of thing, you should at least go for the real thing – like the scary Ms Robinson – rather than bottle-redheads like Sharon Osbourne.

RED
CORNER

'I'm going to beat you like a red-haired stepchild.'
Southern US saying

ginger stereotypes

If you want to combat pigment-stigma, you need to understand the preconceptions people may display when they see your orange tresses. How well do these stereotypical ginger traits describe you?

Fiery temper

Hotheadedness is perhaps the trait most commonly associated with ginners. This is quite an easy claim to find evidence for, because if you accuse someone of being hot-tempered for long enough they'll eventually snap. This was the principle behind 'ginger rage', a mythical condition that playground bullies would attempt to invoke in red-haired kids. To cause it, they'd repeat gingerist insults until the victim got angry. They would then cite this anger as evidence of 'ginger rage'.

Evidence for: Rob Roy, Anne of Green Gables, ginger cats

Evidence against: Non-fiery redhead Steve Davis

Fickleness

Gingers are often regarded as unpredictable, erratic and liable to change their minds. In Susanna Clarke's novel *Jonathan Strange and Mr Norrell*, the magician Mr Norrell complains that 'reddish-brown is such a fickle colour'. Again, this is quite an easy trait to find proof for when you're looking for it.

Evidence for: Royal commitment-phobe Henry VIII, Chris Evans failing to turn up for his Virgin Radio breakfast show

Evidence against: Lenin, Trotsky, Churchill, Scargill, Malcolm X and Boudicca were all ginners who stood firmly by their beliefs

Untrustworthiness

Ever wondered why nobody asks you to mind their bag while they go to the toilet? Feel like it's always you who gets picked out at customs? It could be because of the notion that ginners shouldn't be trusted, which is rooted in red-haired depictions of Judas. Either that or your eyes are too close together.

Evidence for: Judas, Satan, James Hewitt

Evidence against: Florence Nightingale, Tintin

Sexual prowess

Gingers are often regarded as passionate and sexually adventurous lovers, and a whole gingerphile subculture has been created in response to the myth. Well, I say 'myth'. While all the other stereotypes associated with gingers are obviously untrue, I think we should let this one pass.

Evidence for: Jessica Rabbit, Marilyn Monroe, Henry VIII

Evidence against: Ginger tennis star Boris Becker. In 2001, Becker was forced to pay $5 million after a DNA test proved that he fathered a child with Russian model Angela Ermakova in a cupboard in London restaurant Nobu. Becker was alleged to have lasted a mere five seconds, which works out at a pricey million dollars per second.

So – excitable, unpredictable, not to be trusted, but great in bed. Does this sound like you?

Probably not, but let's not get too upset about the ginger stereotype. As anyone who's heard a blonde joke knows, it could be much, much worse.

the ginger hall of shame: notorious gingerphobes

Knowing your enemy is the key to surviving in our carrotphobic world. This section deals with those hair bigots who've fanned the flames of hatred. Remember, they despise you and all your kind. If you see them, confront them and demand an apology.

Aristotle

He may have laid the foundations for Western philosophy, but Aristotle also laid the foundations for gingerphobia. In *Physiognomics*, he claimed that people with tawny coloured hair are brave because they have the same hair colour as lions, while the 'reddish' are of bad character because they have the same hair colour as foxes.

So basically, you can't trust gingas because they look a bit like foxes. And he was supposed to be one of the cleverest people *ever*.

The Bear – *Bo' Selecta!*

In the Channel 4 shows *Bo' Selecta!* and *A Bear's Tail*, coppertopped comic Leigh Francis dresses up as a bear and slings insults like 'ginger bastard' and 'ginger twat' at a red squirrel called Stephen. The red-haired community remains divided over whether Francis is exposing carrotphobic attitudes or whether he's a traitorous self-hating ginge.

Children's BBC

In John Cunliffe's original books, Postman Pat was a ginge. So why did Pat mysteriously become a brunette when the series transferred to Children's BBC in 1981? Refuse to pay your licence fee until there's a ginger remake.

Frank Dobson, MP

When Chris Evans announced that he was donating £100,000 to Ken Livingstone's mayoral campaign fund in 2000, Labour candidate Frank Dobson quipped that he was relieved because his mum had always told him to steer clear of redheads. Evans responded by doubling his donation.

This charge of untrustworthiness is pretty hard to take from someone who is not just a politician, but a beardy one. Also, you have to wonder what the response would have been if Dobson had chosen any other minority group to pick on.

Eric Cartman – *South Park*

Shortly after Dobson's outburst, fellow heavyweight Eric Cartman also spoke out against redheads, claiming that gingerness is a curse that will envelop the earth in blackness for all eternity unless it's wiped out. Unlike Dobson, however, Cartman openly hates all minorities and doesn't belong to a party that has a vision of 'an equal, inclusive society where every citizen is treated with respect' (according to the Labour Party website).

Grey squirrels

Greedy animals who've recently been stealing resources from ginger squirrels and severely affecting their survival rates (see the 'Ginger Creatures' chapter). These fat, acorn-thieving bastards have got to be stopped before it's too late.

npower

Complaints were made to the Advertising Standards Authority in 2000 when the energy supplier npower ran a gingerist ad campaign. The first execution featured a grumpy ginger child next to his ginger parents with the line, 'There are some things in life you can't choose.' The second featured a redheaded bloke looking despondently down his pants at his pubes. As ever with this sort of thing, the resulting press coverage effectively gave npower ad space they didn't have to pay for, which is also what I'm doing now. So I'll stop.

Viz

In 1992, *Viz* comic ran a spoof story detailing how scientists had developed technology to identify red-haired babies in the womb so they can be aborted rather than born with the terrible affliction of gingerness. But *Viz* co-founder Simon Donald is a ginge himself, so we should probably take this as a satirical commentary on society's gingerphobic attitudes.

RED CORNER

'The media always call me ginger in a derogatory manner and I've come to find it very offensive indeed. It's racist.'
Mick Hucknall

the ginger hall of fame:
movie gingers

Marilyn Monroe may have had to dye her ginger hair blonde to achieve fame, but there are many screen icons who made it without hiding their true carrotness.

Woody Allen

Perhaps the greatest ginger filmmaker ever, Allen has been nominated in the 'Best Original Screenplay' category of the Oscars more than anyone else. With his unkempt red hair and thick-rimmed glasses, Allen was the godfather of ginger geek chic, inspiring Dennis Pennis, The Proclaimers and Beaker from *The Muppet Show*.

Ewan McGregor

The Scottish actor has demonstrated remarkable versatility throughout his career, as has his red hair. Few fans will forget its appearance as 'long ginger hair' in *Shallow Grave*, 'ginger crew cut' in *Trainspotting* and, most movingly, 'spiky ginger hair with a rat's tail' in *Star Wars: Episode 1 – The Phantom Menace*.

Nicole Kidman

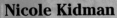

Although she's possibly the most famous ginge in the world, Kidman was only awarded the best actress Oscar when she donned a brunette wig to play Virginia Woolf in *The Hours*. But despite the Academy's clear gingerist bias, Kidman remains a true ginner style icon, with many red-haired women around the world copying the hairstyles that her full-time personal hairdresser creates. Few, however, would want to copy the frizzy ginger perm she sported in debut movie *BMX Bandits*.

Julianne Moore

The star of *Far From Heaven*, *The Hours* and *Magnolia* is not just a critically acclaimed actress, but also a proper ginge with freckles and the kind of translucent skin that must be a bit of a nuisance if you spend a lot of time in LA.

Robert Redford

Ginger heart-throb who has starred in, among others, *All The President's Men*, *Butch Cassidy And The Sundance Kid* and *Indecent Proposal*, in which he offers Demi Moore a million dollars to sleep with him. Most girls round my way would do it for a couple of Bacardi Breezers and the bus fare home.

Molly Ringwald

The eighties were certainly a good time for gingers. Sonia, T'Pau and Tiffany were in the charts, Clive Sinclair was at the cutting edge of technology and ginger teen-movie queen Molly Ringwald ruled the box office. Ringwald's best movie, *The Breakfast Club*, managed to fit in the obligatory eighties dancing sequence despite being set in a Saturday-morning detention class. Amazing.

Julia Roberts

The first actress to command more than $20 million for a film, Julia Roberts has natural auburn hair. She was either making a feminist statement or had run out of razors when she flashed her underarm hair at the paparazzi in 1999, although the hair itself was disappointingly unginger.

Shirley Temple

We all love a ginger child star, whether it's Lena Zavaroni from *Opportunity Knocks*, Lindsay Lohan in *The Parent Trap* or Rupert Grint in the Harry Potter films. But the biggest ginger child star of them all was undoubtedly Shirley Temple, whose dimples and strawberry-blonde curls remain an iconic image. Unfortunately, like so many child stars, Temple met a tragic fate later in life. She became a Republican politician.

the milkman joke

Warning: This section contains the hilarious milkman joke. If you read this section while eating you could be at risk of choking.

There are few jokes that have brought as much pleasure to gingers over the years as this one.

There are two basic requirements for the joke:

1. Two parents who are both non-ginger, but carry the ginger gene.

2. A child who has ginger hair as a result of the above.

Now all you'll need is for every single person who visits the family to notice that the child has hair of a different colour from their parents and say something along the lines of 'How's that ginger milkman these days?' or 'Still got that ginger milkman, have you?'

This might not seem very funny, but it should be remembered that back in the seventies, promiscuous milkmen were considered so side-splitting that they inspired a film called *Confessions Of A Milkman*, a sitcom called *Bottle Boys* and even a number-one single, by Benny Hill, called 'Ernie (The Fastest Milkman In The West)'.

While the subsequent decline of the milk-delivery industry has seen the joke lose much of its hilarious impact, it's still told today for the sake of tradition. The milkman joke has undergone a revival in recent years due to persistent rumours about the parentage of Prince Harry, although here the word 'milkman' is replaced with 'caddish tone-deaf z-list celebrity love rat'.

the ginger hall of fame:
the top ten pop gingers

A pop history without gingerness is simply unthinkable. Imagine a world without Noddy Holder shouting about Christmas, Axl Rose screeching as if he's got his fingers trapped in Heaven's door and that one from Girls Aloud doing whatever it is she does.

So to celebrate the history of ginger popular music, it's time to run down the chart from number ten to number one in true 'Fluff' Freeman style . . .

10: Gina G

Redheaded Australian pop star who represented Britain in the Eurovision Song Contest in 1996. Finished a disappointing seventh with 'Ooh Aah . . . Just A Little Bit', but still managed to make the song a huge international hit. She might fall into the 'ginger one-hit wonder' category, but anyone whose name is an anagram of 'ginga' surely deserves a place in this Hall of Fame.

9: Nicola Roberts – Girls Aloud

Ginger girl-band star who often gets overlooked in favour of Cheryl Tweedy and Sarah Harding in videos and photo shoots. This is either due to anti-ginger prejudice or the fact that she looks about as enthusiastic as the Saturday assistant in your local Poundstretcher.

8: Carol Decker – T'Pau

No one can deny that the eighties were the golden era for female ginger pop. We had Cathy Dennis, Belinda Carlisle, Sonia, Tiffany, Kirsty McColl, Eddi Reader from Fairground Attraction and even Annie Lennox reaching for the hair dye to get in on the carrot pop boom. But gingerest of all was Carol Decker, whose group T'Pau hit number one with 'China In Your Hand' back in 1987.

7: Vivian Stanshall – The Bonzo Dog Doo-Dah Band

Along with his band, Stanshall tasted brief success with novelty hit 'I'm The Urban Spaceman' in 1968, although its B-side, 'Canyons Of Your Mind', was more typical of his jazzy surrealism. A genuine British eccentric, Stanshall sported some of the most extreme ginger hairstyles ever seen during his thirty-year career, including long ginger hair with a side parting, the ginger comb-over, and a sinister bald-head-and-pointy-ginger-beard combo.

6: Axl Rose

Ginger rocker who was born William Bailey, but later changed his name to an anagram of 'oral sex' and fronted Guns N' Roses. A leading figure in the eighties 'hair metal' scene, Rose started out with a frighteningly large ginger 'do that must have taken a shopping-basket full of hairspray to create. These days he can be seen performing live with the spectacularly unwise combination of ginger cornrows and a goatee beard.

Still, Rose proved once and for all that ginners can rock, a lesson which hasn't been lost on Josh Homme from Queens of the Stone Age or Ricky Wilson from Kaiser Chiefs.

5: Van Morrison

Morrison's experimental fusion of jazz, soul and folk has made him one of the most critically adored acts ever, with *Moondance* and *Astral Weeks* frequently turning up in those 'greatest album ever' polls that music magazines run every two weeks or so. Morrison's ginger hairstyles have been no less experimental, if somewhat less acclaimed. He started out with a ginger bob in the sixties, went for a side parting and ginger beard in the seventies before settling on a wispy comb-over for most of the eighties.

4: Rick Astley

Auburn-quiffed singer who was discovered in the eighties by super-producers Stock, Aitken and Waterman, hitting the number-one spot with 'Never Gonna Give You Up'. Rumours that Astley didn't really exist, and that his records were just created by a computer slowing down Kylie Minogue's voice proved to be untrue, and Astley even managed a comeback in the early nineties with the ballad 'Cry For Help'.

3: Noddy Holder – Slade

Ginger brummie with massive sideburns who became an unlikely rock god. Holder and Slade had hits such as 'Coz I Luv You', 'Cum On Feel The Noise' and 'Mama Weer All Crazee Now' in the pre-punk years, when deliberately misspelling words was about as far as rock rebellion went.

2: Art Garfunkel

Not only was Garfunkel one of the most talented people in Simon and Garfunkel, but he also pioneered the daring 'ginger afro' hairstyle. Perhaps the lesson we should take from Art's example is that if you're going to have a strange hairstyle, at least stand next to someone with an obvious toupee, so they get all the hair jibes instead.

And the all-time gingerest pop star is . . .

1: Mick Hucknall – Simply Red

Although he's already triumphed in the 'Ginger Sex Symbol' section of the Hall of Fame, it would be impossible to name anyone else as the top pop coppertop. Hucknall is so ginger he even named his band after his hair colour.

Mick incurs the wrath of the gingerist media for dating an endless succession of beautiful women, but at least he has the respect of the ginger community. After all, if every ginner lived his lifestyle, the gene would have much less chance of dying out.

gingerness in literature

Ginger hair features in the work of some of the greatest writers in the history of the English language, such as Chaucer and Shakespeare. It also features in the work of Dan Brown, who's regarded as one of the greatest writers in the history of the English language by people who still have to say the words out loud as they read.

If you need to bone up on the rich literary heritage of redheads, here's a quick guide.

The Canterbury Tales – Geoffrey Chaucer

Chaucer uses the gingerist connection between red hair and foxes when describing the Miller in the Prologue to *The Canterbury Tales*, stating that: 'His berd, as any sowe or fox was reed.' Come on Geoffrey – if you're going to have a go at gingers, at least bother to run a spell check.

As You Like It – William Shakespeare

At first there seems to be some gingerism in the Bard's work. In *As You Like It*, Rosalind describes Orlando's hair as 'of the dissembling colour', and it's later described as 'something browner than Judas's'. But many portraits seem to show that Shakespeare was a coppertop himself. So was he exposing the gingerphobic conventions of the day, or was he a self-hating ginge?

'The Red-Headed League' – Sir Arthur Conan Doyle

In this classic Sherlock Holmes story, ginger pawnbroker Jabez Wilson gets paid large amounts of money by an organization called 'The Red-Headed League' to copy out passages from the *Encyclopaedia Britannica*. But what is this mysterious association? A Masonic secret society? A ginger supremacist group?

No. Holmes can see the League for what it is – a ginger herring devised to throw him off the scent of an imminent bank robbery. Which is quite rational for a cokehead.

Ulysses – James Joyce

In *Ulysses*, Buck Mulligan claims that 'redheaded women buck like goats,' echoing the themes of less highbrow but more enjoyable works such as *Red-Hot Redheads* and *Raunchy Redheads 3*.

Pippi Longstocking – Astrid Lindgren

Swedish author Astrid Lindgren wrote four books featuring ginger heroine Pippi Longstocking between 1944 and 1959. Pippi had large red pigtails that stuck out from her head at ninety-degree angles, which must surely count alongside the Art Garfunkel afro and the Ziggy Stardust mullet as one of *the* iconic ginger hairstyles.

Tintin – Hergé

Many red-haired comic-strip characters achieved fame in the early twentieth century, with Archie Andrews, Brenda Starr and Little Orphan Annie in the US and Ginger Meggs in Australia. But remarkably, it was Belgium that produced the best of the lot with Tintin. Admittedly, Hergé's ginger journalist himself was duller than the surrounding cast of the Thomson Twins, Captain Haddock and Professor Calculus. But mad props nonetheless to Hergé for creating a carrot top who ranks alongside Plastic Bertrand and Jean Claude Van Damme as one of the few famous Belgians.

The Harry Potter series – J. K. Rowling

As well as being a coppertop herself, Rowling has done her bit to combat gingerphobia by creating an entire family of orange-haired icons – the Weasleys. This still doesn't mean we have to forgive her (or her publisher) for inventing adult editions of children's books, though.

The Da Vinci Code – Dan Brown

Ginger hair plays an important part in Dan Brown's blockbusting novel, and even foreshadows one of the plot twists, so skip this section if you're one of the three remaining people who haven't read it yet.

Female lead Sophie Neveu is described as having 'burgundy' hair at the beginning of the novel, while depictions of Mary Magdalene with red hair are referred to throughout. Towards the end of the book, we meet Sophie's brother, who's described as having 'strawberry-blonde' hair. In the novel's final twist, we discover that Sophie and her brother are red-haired because they're the direct descendants of Mary Magdalene and Christ.

The novel concludes that the Catholic Church has made deliberate attempts to hide this bloodline because it fears the power of the Sacred Feminine. It could just be that they're embarrassed that the descendants of Christ turned out to be carrot tops, though.

Jonathan Strange and Mr Norrell – Susanna Clarke

Some copper-noddled readers wondered if Susanna Clarke's 2004 bestseller *Jonathan Strange and Mr Norrell* represented a return to literary gingerism. In it the narrator states that magician Jonathan Strange's hair 'had a reddish tinge and, as everybody knows, no one with red hair can be said to be truly handsome'. In Clarke's defence, however, it should be noted that the book is set in the early 1800s, well before the birth of Hucknall.

RED CORNER

'You'd find it easier to be bad than good if you had red hair.'

Anne Shirley, Anne of Green Gables, *L. M. Montgomery*

the ginger hall of shame: ginger villains

Not every redhead has made a contribution that we should celebrate. Below is a list of those the ginger community would rather forget about. Go and buy some brown hair dye, guys – you are officially disowned.

Jim Davidson

Comic who mysteriously survived the mid-eighties cull of mainstream comedians and still has a career today.

The Devil

Red-skinned embodiment of evil, the ruler of Hell and the cause of all the suffering in the world.

Judas Iscariot

Pal of Jesus who was often depicted in art as redheaded, inspiring the stereotype of untrustworthy gingers. One of those people who was such a twat that he ruined a perfectly good name for ever – hardly anybody calls their child 'Judas' these days.

Auric Goldfinger – *Goldfinger*

Ginger Bond baddie who plotted to steal the US gold reserve by detonating a nuclear weapon in Fort Knox. Anyone who stood in his way would have to face a Korean man throwing hats. Failed, unsurprisingly.

Nero

Ginger Roman emperor who fed Christians to lions, ordered crucifixions and executed his relatives. The perfect bloke to name a chain of coffee shops after, then. According to popular belief, Nero played his fiddle while Rome burnt. But as the fiddle hadn't been invented by the time of the great fire of Rome, this is probably guff.

Charles Dance

Like so many British actors, Dance makes a living out of being a Hollywood baddie. Roles have included an evil sorcerer in *The Golden Child*, an evil hitman in *The Last Action Hero* and an evil Chancellor of the Exchequer in *Ali G Indahouse*. Much as you have to admire Dance's thespian skills, he's done little to put a positive image of gingerness out there.

Ronald McDonald

The multinational burger chain has used frightening red-haired clown Ronald McDonald as its mascot since 1963. In recent years he's become a hate figure for the anti-globalization movement. But it should be said in his defence that he's caught many food-themed criminals over the years, and if it wasn't for his restaurant chain there would be no public toilets left on the high street at all.

Lizzie Borden

Ginger spinster from New England who, in the late nineteenth century, was accused of the brutal axe murders of her father and stepmother. Although she was acquitted, Borden was widely regarded as guilty, making her the ginger O. J. Simpson. Was she unfairly persecuted by a gingerphobic society, or was she let off to avoid unrest in the redhead community?

Shylock – *The Merchant of Venice*

Evil Jewish moneylender from Shakespeare's *The Merchant of Venice* who tried to extract a pound of flesh from the merchant Antonio when he couldn't repay a debt. In contemporary productions, Shylock would wear a red wig to suggest a connection with Judas and the Devil. Modern productions tend to portray Shylock more sympathetically, although this is probably more to do with concerns about anti-Semitism rather than gingerism.

Major James Hewitt

Ginger cad who had an affair with Princess Di and spilled the beans to the tabloids. Purely because he wanted to get his side of the story across, of course. Not for the cash. Hewitt was subsequently branded as the most evil person in the world by all the tabloids who'd been outbid for the story.

RED CORNER

'Out of the ash
I rise with my red hair
And I eat men like air'
*'Lady Lazarus',
Sylvia Plath*

ginger folklore

Gingers have often been regarded as mysterious and supernatural, which might explain why so many superstitions have developed around them. Have you ever been blanked on New Year's Eve? Was your last holiday to Corsica an unpleasant experience? Here's why.

An old Irish superstition states that if the first person you see after the stroke of midnight on New Year's Eve is ginger, you'll have bad luck all year. Which means that Channel 4 put all our lives at risk when they got Chris Evans to host their 1997 New Year's Eve special. I can't remember anything that bad happening the following year, though. Except possibly the invention of microscooters.

An old wives' tale claims that if you shave ginger hair off, it will grow back darker. This sounds like the kind of excuse that ginger traitors like Tim Culley from *Big Brother 3* would come up with to explain why their hair has mysteriously transformed from ginger to black.

There's also the urban myth that states that red hair is caused by women having sex when they're having their periods. For some reason, this is yet to unseat the Melanocortin-1 receptor theory in scientific circles.

An old superstition reckons that if you wash your hands in the early morning dew on May Day, you can wipe the freckles off your face. Anyone who dislikes their freckles is welcome to try this, though I suspect they'll be just as freckly afterwards, but also a bit cold and tired.

In the nineteenth century it was widely believed that ginners brought bad luck to ships and there are recorded examples of crews refusing to sail with redheads on board. Hang on a minute . . . Didn't Kate Winslet have red hair in *Titanic*? Perhaps they were on to something.

In Corsica, gingers are apparently considered such bad luck that if you pass one on the street you should spit and turn around. But despite their superstition, Corsicans are happy to promote their island as the birthplace of fiery ginge Napoleon Bonaparte. The hypocrites.

Not all folklore depicts gingers in an unfavourable light. An old Scottish superstition claims that if you rub your hand on a ginger's head, you'll be brought good luck. I'd advise getting permission before trying this, though. I can't imagine that walking into a Glasgow pub and giving a hard ginger bloke a noogie will bring you much luck.

Gingers are regarded as most lucky of all, however, in Poland, where a tradition claims that you'll become rich if you pass three redheads on the run. God knows what kind of chaos would have ensued if the Partridge Family had toured there.

RED CORNER

'If you want trouble, find yourself a redhead.'

US saying

the ginger hall of fame:
tv gingers

Ever since the invention of colour TV, we've demanded a constant stream of orange-noggined stars on our screens to show off the technology to full effect. But which of them deserve ginger immortality?

Les Battersby-Brown – *Coronation Street*
Actor Bruce Jones started out in gritty and realistic Ken Loach film *Raining Stones* before finding regular employment in *Coronation Street*, which could only be less gritty and realistic if the characters had special powers.

Basil Brush
Ginger puppet who's been a kid's TV staple since the early seventies. Brush was both posh and a fox, so he must have been quite confused about whether to join the Countryside Alliance or not.

Bianca – *EastEnders*
Ginge actress Patsy Palmer played Bianca in *EastEnders* between 1993 and 1999. During this time, anyone called 'Ricky' would have their name shouted at them in imitation of her screeching cockney voice,

in much the same way that anyone called 'Elliot' had their name shouted at them in ET's voice in 1982.

Since leaving *EastEnders*, Palmer has produced the exercise DVD *Ibiza Workout*, which presumably aims to give you the same urge for vigorous movement as someone who's just necked four Ecstasy tabs.

Charlie Dimmock

The *Ground Force* star did little to challenge wanton redhead stereotypes when she invented braless gardening in 1998. Whether this was intended as a feminist statement or a ratings-boosting stunt, it gave a generation of adolescent boys the kind of pre-watershed thrills they'd only previously been able to get from women's beach volleyball and *Baywatch*.

Chris Evans

Presenter and DJ who fronted *The Big Breakfast*, *TFI Friday* and *Don't Forget Your Toothbrush*. The tabloids dubbed Evans 'the ginger binger' on account of his marathon boozing sessions, and 'the ginger whinger' when he moaned about getting sacked by Virgin Radio as a result.

Bamber Gascoigne

The original presenter of *University Challenge*, Bamber Gascoigne was like the chummy supply teacher to Jeremy Paxman's strict headmaster. He didn't shout at you if you got it wrong, but that only made you feel more disappointed with yourself.

Leigh Francis

The star of lewd mask comedy *Bo' Selecta!*, which features characters such as Eastern European celebrity stalker Avid Merrion, and a gingerphobic bear (see page 52). In 2005, Craig David claimed that Francis's surreal caricature of him helped to kill his career. Although why anyone who specializes in dull R&B ballads with Spanish guitar backing would need any help in killing their career, I don't know.

Bonnie Langford

Started out in *Just William* threatening to thkweam and thkweam and thkweam until she was thick. Then became a Doctor Who assistant and thkweamed until *we* all were.

Nicholas Witchell

The ginger face of BBC news, Witchell was chosen as the first frontman of *The Six O'Clock News* when it launched in 1984. Witchell himself became news in 1988 when lesbians protesting against Clause 28 invaded the studio. He demonstrated his ginger ninja credentials by heroically sitting on one of them to restrain her.

ginger sexism

One of the more unfortunate aspects of gingerism is that it seems to affect blokes more than women. For some reason, ginger women are perceived as sexy, mysterious and dangerous while ginger blokes are thought of as a bit sad.

This inequality is even reflected in the language we use to describe coppertops. The word 'redhead' is likely to conjure up an image of a mysterious femme fatale, while the word 'ginger' suggests a carrot-topped bloke.

'Redheads'	'Gingers'
Julianne Moore	Chris Evans
Nicole Kidman	Steve Davis
Jessica Rabbit	Rick Astley
Rita Hayworth	James Hewitt
Gillian Anderson	Ron Weasley

By the same token, if you ordered a specialist DVD called something like *Red-Hot Redheads* over the Internet, you'd probably feel a bit short-changed if the redheads in question were pasty ginger blokes.

Coppertopped author Tom Robbins writes about this inequality in his 1988 essay 'Ode to Redheads'. He claims that while ginger blokes look like 'brown-haired men who've been composted', ginger women wear their hair 'like a tiara of rubies'.

Add to this the difficulty of finding acceptable ginger facial hair and it does seem that ginger blokes have it tougher. But before we get too upset about this inequality, let's remember that if Mick Hucknall can become a worldwide sex symbol, there's hope for all of us.

ginger faq

Are gingers less likely to go grey?

In a way. Greying is caused when the body stops producing melanin, which causes hair to lose its colour. However, when this process occurs in ginger hair, it tends to look blonde rather than grey.

the ginger hall of fame: ginger creatures

The ancient Egyptians believed that all red animals were evil and in league with the evil god Set. And it's difficult to disagree with this when you look at Cuddles from *The Keith Harris Show*. But there are some ginger creatures who deserve their place alongside the humans in our Hall of Fame.

Foxes

As detailed in the 'Notorious Gingerphobes' chapter, the association between foxes and gingers has been made since the days of Aristotle. And while they've traditionally been depicted as cunning and duplicitous, many modern foxes, such as Basil Brush, Fantastic Mr Fox and Disney's Robin Hood, have worked hard to overturn the stereotype, and the ginger community can now take the comparison as a compliment.

Goldfish

Small, orange members of the carp family often given away in water-filled plastic bags as fairground prizes. Goldfish make quite rubbish prizes as you either have to go out and buy a tank or carry the bag around for ever. But for their contribution to office receptions and dentists' waiting rooms everywhere, goldfish should be welcomed into the Hall of Fame. Even though they'll forget about it in seven seconds' time.

Cats (ginger)

Mark Twain famously claimed that while the rest of the human race is descended from apes, redheads are descended from cats.

Certainly, cats and gingers are both perceived to be fickle and a bit supernatural. But it's rare for human gingers to mark boundaries with urine or lick their own genitals in public, so I think I'll have to differ with Twain on this one.

Highland cattle

Until the late nineteenth century, Highland cattle in the black and brown varieties were more common. However, Queen Victoria liked the ginger ones so much that she issued a royal decree ensuring that they were selectively bred to encourage the orange colour. Well, at least they match the people now.

Red squirrels

Remember when squirrels used to be sweet? Remember how they used to have bushy tails, tufty ears and cute little faces?

That was back in the days when they were ginger. Then the bigger, stronger grey squirrels came along, stole all their acorns, and caused the survival rates of red squirrels to plummet. Now all we're left with are those vicious grey bastards who would mug old ladies for their sandwiches if they had opposable thumbs.

Perhaps the animal kingdom is trying to tell us something here – let the gingers die out and it's bad news for everyone.

Robin redbreasts

Ginger-fronted birds that are often seen hanging around in gardens looking for worms, building nests in discarded kettles and posing for Christmas cards.

Yellow lab mice

This might seem a strange entry in a list of ginger animals, but it was through American scientist Roger Cone's experiments on yellow laboratory mice that the 'ginger gene', the Melanocortin-1 receptor, was discovered. Apparently, this gene underlies the presence of yellow hair in mice and red hair in humans, so it's only fair to make them honorary gingers in this Hall of Fame.

the ginger buyer's guide

Many redheads these days take refuge from our cruel gingerist world with a spot of retail therapy. Responding to this, thousands of companies are chasing 'the orange pound'. But what are the iconic ginger products that should make it on to your shopping list?

Wotsits

Of all the bright orange corn snacks of the early eighties – Griddles, Space Raiders, Puffs – there was only ever going to be one winner. Wotsits were superior partly because you could lick the ends and stick them together to make sculptures, partly because they made your very fingers turn orange, and partly because they were so overloaded with flavouring that it would often form itself into hard lumps at the bottom of the pack.

Tango

This iconic orange drink has a history of ginger advertising mascots. The most notorious campaign ran in the early nineties, and featured the fat orange man with a nappy who would slap people on both sides of the head when they took a sip. Unfortunately, the ads led to a spate of copycat behaviour in playgrounds, much of which was directed at ginners on the grounds that their hair was proof that they'd already 'been Tango'd'.

Carrots

The vegetable that will be forever associated with gingers. Interestingly, the first recorded carrots were not orange at all, but purple, white, yellow, black and green, and the orange carrot we know today was not developed until the eighteenth century. You could try pointing this out next time someone calls you 'carrot top' but I've got a feeling you might be digging yourself in deeper.

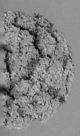

McVities' Ginger Nuts

The undisputed kings of the ginger biscuit world, McVities' Ginger Nuts actually have enough ginger in them to taste quite hot. You should therefore remember to be extra cautious around them, as in severe cases they can lead to you drinking more tea than you'd originally planned.

Jaffa Cakes

The debate about whether these are cakes or biscuits has raged for decades and is unlikely to be resolved in any of our lifetimes. But whatever classification you favour, the 'smashing orangey bit' means they'll always be an iconic ginger brand.

Swan Vestas

Brand of matches that inspired a nickname for gingers on account of their pale bodies, red tops and fieriness.

Ginger beer

Soft drink that once enjoyed a high level of popularity with children because it has the word 'beer' in its name. However, the playground credibility of the drink nosedived when 'ginger beer' caught on as rhyming slang for 'queer'.

Irn-Bru

Orange soft drink that's popular with the Scots. But so are deep-fried chocolate bars, offal and heroin, so it's not really much of an endorsement.

the ginger hall of shame: ginger scandals

Whether it's Chris Evans making a few more million quid, Nicole Kidman's relationships or insinuations about Prince Harry's parentage, coppertops are rarely out of the red-tops these days. Here are some of the gingas who've provided the biggest tabloid scoops.

Geri Halliwell and Chris Evans

Britain's two most famous gingers sparked a celeb-mag frenzy when they were seen around together for a few months in 1999. Some speculated that we could be about to witness the biggest ginger wedding of all time. Others wondered why the romance blossomed at the exact time Halliwell had a new album out.

Neil Kinnock

Following Labour's defeat in the 1992 general election, there was some suggestion in the tabloids that Kinnock's colour might have contributed to his defeat. Is Britain really so gingerphobic that it would vote for John Major just to avoid having a carrot in charge?

It's unlikely. The statistics show that a ginger coalition between Kinnock and strawberry-blonde Paddy Ashdown would have gained enough votes to win the election, so hair colour probably wasn't a factor. Footage of Kinnock punching the air and shouting 'Well alright! Well alright!' in an embarrassing disco-vicar style just before the election might have been, though.

Malcolm McLaren

Ginger rock manager Malcolm McLaren engineered many tabloid scandals to promote The Sex Pistols in the late seventies. The most famous was when the Pistols outraged a nation with rude words like 'fucker', 'bastard' and 'rotter' on *The Bill Grundy Show* in 1976.

After inventing punk, McLaren shocked the world further by inventing skipping with two ropes at a time. His own top-ten hits, 'Buffalo Girls' and 'Double Dutch', mark him out as not so much the greatest ginger hip-hop star ever as the *only* ginger hip-hop star ever.

Anne Robinson

Robinson caused a tabloid furore in 2001 when she made derogatory comments about the Welsh on the TV show *Room 101*. Come on guys, these ginge-on-ginge attacks have to stop.

Rebekah Wade

Ginger editor of *The Sun*. Played up to feisty ginger stereotypes in 2005 by battering boyfriend Ross 'Grant Mitchell off *EastEnders*' Kemp. Oddly, *The Sun* gave the story much less coverage than other tabloids the following day.

James Hewitt and Prince Harry

In a tabloid variation of the milkman joke (see page 58), much has been made over the years of the fact that Princess Diana's former lover and Prince Harry both have ginger hair.

ginger faq

Are gingers more likely to be left wing?

It would seem so. The history of politics is littered with those who were red in more than one way. After all, Lenin and Trotsky were both ginners, and both favoured the kind of orange goatee still seen on many politics students today. At the height of the Thatcherite eighties, opposition came from ginger comb-over merchants Arthur Scargill and Neil Kinnock. Tellingly, the Labour party veered sharply to the right when brunette Tony Blair took over in the nineties, rendering boozy ginge Charles Kennedy's Liberal Democrats the most left wing of the three major parties.

ginger fashion dos

It's difficult enough being a ginge in today's shallow world without fashion disasters exacerbating matters. But as the many redheaded Hollywood stars can attest, it *is* possible to choose clothes that look fabulous with your distinctive tresses, especially if you have a personal stylist, unlimited budget and Miuccia Prada's private phone number. Just in case you don't, here are a few basic pointers (aimed primarily at women – unless you're a ginger man *and* a transvestite. In which case, God help you.)

Do choose clothes in 'cool' colours to balance out the red hair. By that we mean cream, earthy brown, sea-green, ivory, denim blue, and so on. As a general rule, steer clear of bright pinks, yellows and reds as they can clash with your hair. If you work in kids' TV, you may wish to consider switching careers.

fashion

Stick to a fairly neutral palette when it comes to makeup. Some olive- or darker-skinned people can get away with electric blue mascara and hot pink blusher. You can't. Get over it. That said, a mossy green eyeshadow or a carefully chosen terracotta lipstick can look good against pale skin and red hair.

Wear your freckles with pride! Freckles are a natural part of the ginger look and many gingerphiles think they're pretty damn sexy too. If you cover them with foundation, you're no better than those traitorous ginners who dye their hair.

ginger fashion don'ts

So there you are, first thing in the morning, half-asleep, pulling on the first clothes you find in your wardrobe. Blearily you look at yourself in the mirror. Ronald McDonald stares back at you. Hell, it's happened to all of us. So what to do when you finally realize your stripy red tights, yellow knee-length dungarees and size 20 shoes just aren't cutting the sartorial mustard any more? The first thing to do is to become your own Fashion Police and arrest all of the following items in your closet:

Bright red clothes
The general rule that's often given to redheads is to avoid matching your clothes to the colour of your hair. It might have worked for Jessica Rabbit, but that's no guarantee it will work for you.

Red lipstick
It's best to avoid bright red lipstick and pale foundation unless you actually want to look like a clown. Not a good look (unless you're a clown).

Red-rimmed glasses

While we're on the subject of avoiding red, going for a pair of eighties-style red-rimmed glasses just because they match the colour of your hair is also a bad idea.

Fake tan

You get enough stick as it is for having orange hair. Do you really want orange skin too? Anyway, we all know that if you actually went out in the sun without your factor 50 on, you'd look like Michael Gambon in *The Singing Detective*, not David Dickinson.

The 'Hip-Hop' look

There are some people who can pull off a baggy tracksuit and a few hundred pounds of bling. It's unlikely, however, that these people are gingers. If you try it, you may end up looking like a strawberry-blonde Jimmy Savile.

ginger hair dos

Much like Mogwai from *Gremlins*, red hair behaves well if you look after it, but can turn into a horrible, snarling monster if you mistreat it.

Ginger hair tends to be dryer than other hair types, so it may be worth trying a moisturizing shampoo. And this goes for redheaded blokes, too. If you're comfortable enough with your masculinity to buy something with the word 'moisturizing' in its name, that is.

Most ginger hair dries out easily in hot weather, so be careful not to stay out in the sun too long. Although if you've got the kind of complexion that most gingers find themselves stuck with, you'll be about as likely to stay out in the sun too long as Nosferatu is.

Air-dry your hair whenever possible. Too much blow-drying can leave it brittle, while rubbing it dry with a towel can cause split ends. Obviously, if you live in the Orkney Islands and you're currently experiencing a bit of a cold snap, don't run out of the house with wet hair. But try and let your hair dry naturally whenever you can.

Try not to wash your hair too often. Once every other day is fine, unless you work in a fish-gutting factory. Ginger hairs are typically thicker than those of other hues, and can get tangled easily. Although it's tempting to thrash tangles out with a brush while your hair's dry, it's better to use a wide-toothed comb after applying a conditioner in the shower.

And finally, keep it away from bright light, don't get it wet, and never, ever feed it after midnight. No, hang on a minute. That's *Gremlins* again.

ginger hair don'ts

Bright orange hair can be more noticeable than other kinds, so ginners should take particular care to avoid bad hairstyles. Increase your chances of succeeding in this hair-colour-prejudiced world by steering clear of the following . . .

Ginger dreads
You might think they make you look like a natty rasta from Kingston Town. Everyone else will think you look like a trust-fund crusty called Jeremy wigging out to a bongo solo at the Glastonbury stone circle.

The ginger pudding bowl
The ginger version of the popular hairstyle that's created when your mum puts an upside-down pudding bowl on your head and snips around it. Playground bullies won't know where to begin if they see one of these.

The ginger afro
Spherical hairstyle, pioneered by Art Garfunkel, that all but disappeared in the eighties and nineties. Happily, it's now enjoying something of a comeback thanks to the influence of John Heder in *Napoleon Dynamite*.

The ginger mullet
The mullet may have made something of an ironic revival recently, but if it's bright ginger, you're probably crossing a line that shouldn't be crossed. Still, ginger mullets were good enough for Ziggy Stardust, Rula Lenska, Chuck Norris, Ewan McGregor in *Attack of the Clones* and Tenderheart Lion from the Care Bear Cousins, so who am I to judge?

The ginger Croydon facelift
The famous chav hairstyle, created by scraping your hair back, sticking a scrunchie on it and fixing it in place with half a can of hairspray. Ginger Croydon facelifts are thankfully quite rare, although a few have been spotted on Scottish council estates. Also known as Scouse Fountains.

The ginger rat's tail
Are you Obi-Wan Kenobi in *Star Wars: Episode I – The Phantom Menace* or Tom Bailey, the lead singer of eighties band The Thompson Twins? No? Then don't even consider going there.

The ginger comb-over
The bald head with a clump of ginger hair swept over it was a much more common sight back in the seventies and eighties. No longer, thank God.

Ginger roots
The Ginger Survival Guide does not condone dyeing your hair. (But if you do indulge in this cowardly act, you could at least do your roots every now and then to avoid looking like a Fry's Orange Cream bar.)

RED CORNER

'It ought to be a criminal offence for women to dye their hair. Especially red. What the devil do they want to do that for?'

Bill, Indiscretions of Archie,
P. G. Wodehouse

98

ginger beards

It's often said that people with beards are untrustworthy, and that they have something to hide. Gingers, too, often face the accusation that because of their hair they are not to be trusted. Combine the two, and it's unlikely you'll be getting many babysitting offers.

Still, most blokes feel the urge to go all beardy and serious at some point in their lives. If you're feeling the need to grow ginger facial hair, here are a few options.

Designer stubble
Not quite sure who the designer was that suggested this, but it's unlikely he had gingers in mind.

Mutton chops
Massive ginger sideburns, as sported by evil butcher Hilary Briss in BBC comedy *The League of Gentlemen*. Facial hair features so terrifying you can actually buy them from joke shops at Halloween.

The goatee beard
Note to students: if you're ginger, growing a triangular beard will not make you look arty and mysterious. It will make you look like Lenin.

The full beard
The complete ginger beard as favoured by Henry VIII and the Nordic god Thor. Quite a good look if you're a king or a god, not such a good look if you work in a call centre in Swindon.

The Van Dyke
The classic goatee and moustache combination that makes redheads look like Satan.

The bumfluff beard
The downy facial hair that teenage boys grow in a vain attempt to get served in pubs. This will be barely noticeable against your skin if you're towards the strawberry-blonde end of the spectrum.

The chin curtain
The beard-but-no-moustache look may be popular with the Amish community, but it's best to steer clear of it if you're a ginge. You'll only look like a leprechaun.

the ginger hall of fame:
ginger beardies

When red-haired women want style tips, they may scour *Heat* magazine for pictures of Julianne Moore or Marcia Cross (who plays the mad obsessive one in *Desperate Housewives*). But which style icons should ginger blokes look to when they're deciding on facial hair? Here are some of history's beardiest ginger icons.

Robin Cook

The late Labour MP was often compared to a garden gnome on account of his tidy ginger beard. But Cook didn't let the taunting affect his confidence, and he even managed to have an affair with his parliamentary assistant.

Ulysses S. Grant

They say you can't trust a ginger beardy. But the Yanks don't believe this – they elected bearded ginge Ulysses S. Grant as president in 1869.

Orang-utans

The largest tree-climbing mammals, orang-utans typically go for the Noddy Holder ginger-sideburns look, although some of the more adventurous ones have full ginger beards.

Noddy Holder

The Slade lead singer's bushy ginger sideburns were so popular in the seventies that the world was given yet another ginger pubes euphemism: 'Noddy Holder's sideburns'.

Obi-Wan Kenobi

Few could have guessed that the mysterious white-haired old man who meets Luke Skywalker in the original Star Wars movie had been a powerful Jedi Master, or that he once had the bright orange mullet and tidybeard we see on Ewan McGregor in *Star Wars: Episode II – Attack of the Clones*.

Alexei Lalas

He has a straggly beard and he likes playing the acoustic guitar. But surprisingly, he's not a politics student – he's a US soccer star.

D. H. Lawrence

The twentieth-century novelist shocked the nation with both *Lady Chatterley's Lover* and his ginger beard and comb-over combination.

Avid Merrion
The stalker comedian sports a perfect ginger example of the clipped square beard known as 'the doorknocker'. Terrifying.

George Bernard Shaw
Dramatist and critic Shaw also toyed with a variety of ginger beards and didn't lose his virginity until he was twenty-nine. I'm not suggesting the two were related.

Vincent Van Gogh
Beardy ginger artist who must have needed to stock up on orange paint before he did all those self-portraits.

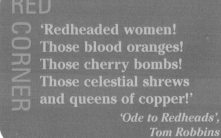

RED CORNER

'Redheaded women! Those blood oranges! Those cherry bombs! Those celestial shrews and queens of copper!'

'Ode to Redheads',
Tom Robbins

oi, baldie!

Is it true that gingers are less likely to go bald than other blokes?

Sadly, no. Thinning hair is less noticeable in gingers, as there isn't as much contrast between hair and scalp colour as with darker mops. But this isn't much consolation when it's all gone, and you only have to look at Ron Howard, Arthur Scargill and Van Morrison to see that this happens to gingers too.

Going prematurely bald seems especially unfair for ginger blokes. As soon as the taunts of 'coppertop' and 'carrot head' stop, the jibes of 'cue ball' and 'chrome dome' start.

Looking on the bright side, though, cropped hair is still in fashion, which means that you needn't go through the hair-loss process looking like Terry Nutkins or Mel Smith.

But what should you do when you start to notice people pointing at you and slapping their foreheads as you pass them in the street?

The most important thing is to avoid worrying. Stress is thought to be one of the biggest causes of hair loss, so avoid panicking at all costs. If you do, you'll only make yourself go bald quicker. I realize I'm probably not helping much here.

Other than moderating your panic, use a mild shampoo and a wide-toothed comb, lay off the hairspray unless you really want to look like Rula Lenska, and avoid getting a ginger perm (in the highly unlikely event that they ever come back into fashion).

Most advice about managing hair loss will also recommend that you avoid dyeing your hair. In this particular case, however, any traitors who attempt to disguise their natural gingerness deserve everything they get, so we'll leave that particular tip to one side.

RED CORNER

'Once in his life, every man is entitled to fall in love with a gorgeous redhead.'

Lucille Ball

the ginger hall of fame:
ginger slapheads

Don't worry if you're getting into the habit of pulling clumps of ginger hair out of the plughole. Take inspiration from those who lived full and successful lives despite losing their flowing, glowing, copper locks.

Elizabeth I

The Tudor monarch's natural ginger hair fell out when she tried to wash it with lye (a strong cleaning solution), and for much of her reign she was a baldie with a ginger wig. Which may possibly explain the whole 'virgin queen' thing.

Napoleon Bonaparte

Napoleon Bonaparte sported long, centre-parted ginger hair in his days as a young army officer, but by the time he came to be Emperor of France it was obviously receding, with the few strands of hair brushed forward from the back fooling no one. Bonaparte attempted to distract attention from this by invading Russia.

Groundskeeper Willie – *The Simpsons*

The Scottish janitor may be noted for his bushy ginger beard, moustache and eyebrows, but on the top of his head he has even fewer hairs than Homer. Two less, in fact. I've counted.

Ron Howard

Howard found fame in the seventies as Ritchie Cunningham in *Happy Days* when he had a neat ginger side parting. He returned to the spotlight a couple of decades later as an Oscar-winning movie director. But by this point hair-parting was no longer an issue.

Van Morrison

Morrison had a couple of bad-hair decades earlier in his career, but he's now joined the ranks of stars who are unlikely to be employing a Nicole-Kidman-style personal hairdresser anytime soon.

Art Garfunkel

Garfunkel bravely decided to stick with his groundbreaking ginger afro hairstyle throughout the seventies, despite a clearly receding hairline. By the time he was back in the charts with 'Bright Eyes', he looked like a bald man with an orange halo.

Arthur Scargill

As the leader of the National Union of Mineworkers throughout the eighties miners' strike, Scargill had one of the most extraordinary ginger comb-overs ever seen. Fortunately for any onlookers, he often covered it up with a miner's helmet as a gesture of solidarity.

Nicholas Witchell

Ginger newsreader whose forehead has gradually been expanding since it first appeared on our screens in the early eighties. He has now joined the ranks of those unfortunate men who only need to take soap into the shower.

ginger skin

This section deals with ginger skin. That's not ginger skin in the David Dickinson or Judith Chalmers sense, but the kind of pale, translucent skin that often comes with ginger hair.

Unlike red hair, pale skin may convey an evolutionary advantage. It has been suggested that in places such as the north of Scotland, pale skin is useful as it absorbs more sunlight and prevents vitamin D deficiency. This in turn prevents rickets, which inhibits childbirth. So nothing to worry Darwin there.

The problem with this kind of skin only became apparent when package holidays to Tenerife were invented and gingers realized that rickets was the least of their worries if they took their pale skin out into the burning midday sun.

But however you got your ginger skin, you're stuck with it. As well as with the jokes about SPF 100 sunblock and getting sunburn from light bulbs.

What are the dangers to ginger skin?

Well, sunburn's a bit of a bugger, obviously. Although some gingerphobes such as Eric Cartman from *South Park* believe that gingers avoid sunlight because they're all vampires, most scientists will tell you it's really to do with how much melanin your skin produces. Dark skin is dark because it has a higher number of melanin-producing cells, and therefore more melanin. When exposed to the sun, it goes darker – rather than burning – for the same reason. Pale skin can't produce melanin as easily, and this lack causes the tissue to burn.

But painful though it is, sunburn isn't the only thing you need to watch out for if you stay in the sun for too long. Pale skin is also more susceptible to the sun's UVA rays, which cause the skin to wrinkle and age prematurely.

Worse still, gingers are among the highest-risk groups for skin cancer. And the risk is even higher if you're female, have lots of moles and freckles, have a history of the disease in your family and have a habit of forgetting your sunblock when you're packing.

What can be done to avoid these dangers?

Get a high-factor suncream. Be on the safe side and go for SPF 30, or even SPF 50 if you're visiting a hot country for the first time. Yes, your more reckless friends may tease, but you can always get your revenge by giving them a sunburn slap later on.

Remember to apply your sunscreen frequently. Don't be lulled into a false sense of security if it clouds over a bit or it looks like the sun's going down. You'll still get burnt if you don't apply a fresh layer. And I don't mean to nag, but check your sunscreen is waterproof before taking a dip in the pool.

GINGER PROTECTION
factor 50

Avoid staying out in the sun in the middle of the day. Yes, I know you want your money's worth from your package deal, but that doesn't mean you have to be outdoors *all* the time. If all the locals disappear for their siestas, leaving just the pink blokes in the Union Jack shorts, it's probably time to head for the shade.

If your skin is especially sensitive to the sun, consider buying clothing that protects you from the sun, such as fingerless gloves and wide-brimmed hats. Just remember to take them off when you go indoors to avoid being mistaken for Michael Jackson.

If this all sounds like a lot of bother, remember that by taking such precautions you'll be protecting your health – and, importantly, you won't end up looking like Dame Barbara Cartland by the time you're thirty.

Freckles

As well as being lumbered with the kind of skin that makes Marilyn Manson look like Jodie Marsh, many gingers also find themselves covered in freckles.

Although pale skin typically produces less melanin than darker skin, some skin cells will still produce it, causing the small, visible patches of melanin known as freckles.

This explains why some gingers go freckly rather than tanned in the sun. The same process of melanin being released into skin cells is occurring, but the distribution is uneven.

Like ginger hair itself, freckles have aroused much superstition throughout history – as a sign that someone was involved in witchcraft, for example. Sadly, however, the stigma surrounding freckles continues in the school playground today, where many children spread the cruel rumour that freckles are a disease that you'll catch if you sit next to a freckly child or borrow their calculator.

There are yet further cruel myths: that freckles are tiny specks of dirt, rust or fly poo that should be scrubbed off your face; that if you touch them they'll rub off on your hand; and, even more preposterously, that a join-the-dots picture will appear if you connect all the freckles on someone's face.

To counter these falsehoods, you may possibly consider telling a ginger child that their freckles are the marks left by an angel who has kissed their face in the middle of the night because the child's been good. However, while this is clearly intended to make a child feel better about their freckles, the thought of anything meddling around with their face in the middle of the night may freak them out. It's probably better to tell them about melanin.

the ginger hall of shame:
fake gingers

In the last few years, red has overtaken blonde as the most popular colour of hair dye. This is partly down to the long-overdue proliferation of ginger fashion icons, and partly because red dyes fade quicker than other types, and hairdressers are always keen to push styles that will incur more repeat visits.

But ginger envy is nothing new. In fact, many of the celebrities we think of as redheads are nothing more than shameless impostors.

Gillian Anderson
Originally blonde, Anderson reached for the red hair dye to secure the role of FBI Agent Dana Scully in *The X Files* and the role of pinup in IT departments across the world.

Cilla Black
The Ronald McDonald-lookalike presenter has sustained the pretence of gingerness for so long that many people wrongly presume she's a natural redhead. But look back to the Cavern-era publicity shots and you'll see that it's all out of a bottle. Or, more accurately, several thousand bottles by now.

David Bowie / Ziggy Stardust

Bowie has taken on many personas over the years, from Thin White Duke to scary clown walking in front of a bulldozer. But perhaps the most famous of all was androgynous alien rock star Ziggy Stardust, who remains to this day the coolest person ever to have a ginger mullet.

Geri Halliwell

Bottle-ginge pop star who helped to invent 'Girl Power', an offshoot of feminism that involved drinking alcopops and shouting.

Looking back, none of the Spice Girls' nicknames were particularly accurate. Ginger wasn't really ginger, Scary wasn't really scary and Posh definitely wasn't posh.

Rita Hayworth

She may have been the archetypal fiery redhead, but Hayworth was actually a brunette who first dyed her hair red to star in a film called *The Strawberry Blonde*. So Rita Hayworth wasn't really a ginger but Marilyn Monroe was? And I thought Hollywood stars weren't *complete* fakes.

Debra Messing

The star of *Will and Grace*, the popular American sitcom about a gay man and a ginger fag hag. But hang on a minute! He's not actually gay and she's not actually ginger. Can we trust these media people about anything?

Intriguingly, when the BBC made its own fag-hag sitcom, *Gimme, Gimme, Gimme*, lead actress Kathy Burke also had red hair. Are ginger girls and ginger beers really so attracted to each other?

Cynthia Nixon

American actress who plays Miranda in *Sex and the City*. She isn't a ginger in real life, but she *is* a lesbian, so she still deserves some minority-group street cred.

Sharon Osbourne

Shazza spent the eighties and nineties as the most powerful frumpy housewife in heavy rock. She then transformed herself into a matriarchal vamp with the simple addition of red hair dye. (And hundreds of thousands of pounds' worth of plastic surgery.)

Sissy Spacek

The US actress has had a long and distinguished ginger career. But in actual fact it's all out of a bottle. And she can't move objects just by looking at them either.

Stelios

Okay, so he doesn't actually dye his hair red, but by building the 'easy' brand he's demonstrated a desire to turn the world orange that can only be interpreted as deep-seated ginger envy. Thanks to Stelios, we now have carrot-coloured planes, Internet cafés, hire cars and, most distastefully of all, cruise ships full of pikeys.

Kate Winslet

Was ginger in *Titanic*, got to shag Leonardo DiCaprio and survived. Was a brunette in *Finding Neverland*, didn't get to shag Johnny Depp and died. Will she ever learn?

ginger faq

Are gingers harder than other people?

The scientific evidence is pretty mixed on this. While a 2005 study by the Medical Research Council's Human Genetics Unit indicated that ginners are less likely to feel pain, a rival study conducted by the University of Kentucky indicated that gingers are actually more susceptible to pain. But who needs scientific evidence when you've got Chuck Norris fighting commies, Boudicca battering Romans and Nicholas Witchell restraining lesbians live on TV? Of *course* ginners are harder.

the ginger travel guide

If you've got the kind of pale skin that typically comes with ginger hair, you're probably not up for frying on a sunlounger in Greece. So what are the best alternative destinations for gingers?

Scotland

With 13 per cent of its population ginners, Scotland boasts the highest percentage of carrot tops anywhere in the world – a ginger spiritual home, if you will. It's also the land of Rob Roy, Minnie the Minx, Groundskeeper Willie, Highland cattle, Irn-Bru and deep-fried chocolate oranges. In fact, there's only one reason why gingers shouldn't visit Scotland for their holidays, and that's if they already live there.

Ireland

Like Scotland, Ireland boasts a sizeable ginger population, and gave us many red-haired icons, including James Joyce, George Bernard Shaw, and leprechauns. Be warned, however, that most of it's further south than Scotland, so pack your SPF 50 sunblock if you're visiting in the summer.

North America

If you want to be regarded as a 'cute redhead' rather than a 'ginger whinger', the US is the place to go. It's home to the world's largest gingerphile community, including Bruce Springsteen and Fred Flintstone. The only problem is that some parts, such as Florida and California, get sunshine all year round. Alaska's pretty nice, though.

Svalbard

This group of freezing islands in the Arctic Ocean has never really caught on as a tourist destination. But with the right investment from package-holiday companies there's absolutely no reason why it couldn't become the ginger Ibiza, where carrot tops could go for their summer holidays without the fear of sunburn.

Greenland

Arctic island nation that was founded by ginger Viking explorer Erik the Red, according to Norse sagas. In an early example of travel-agent spin, Erik apparently gave it the appealing name 'Greenland' to attract more settlers. Reasonable, as 'freezing lump of ice near the North Pole' probably didn't have the same ring to it. Still, you'll be pretty safe from sunburn here, too.

The North Pole

Seeing a pattern here? If you've tried Iceland, Greenland and Svalbard and they were a bit on the hot side, consider an expedition to the North Pole. The chances of sunburn are especially slim in the winter, when it's dark for twenty-four hours a day. Just don't be surprised if a few of your toes stay in your socks when you take them off.

advice for ginger wannabes

'Are you sick of your hair colour?' asks an ad for red hair dye. 'Make a statement. Shock them. Go red.'

It doesn't seem fair. None of these wannabe ginners had to put up with all the schoolyard jibes about ginger nuts and Ronald McDonald. But now that gingerness is trendy, they want in.

Well, they'll never be anything more than pigmentary tourists. They'll never truly understand the struggle of the gingers. Still, if you're a blonde- or dark-haired person, and you want to hop on the flaming bandwagon, here's a brief guide to going ginge without exposing yourself as a shameless impostor.

First, decide between hair dye and henna. Hair dye provides a more convincing shade of gingerness while henna only turns you from blonde to strawberry blonde or from brunette to auburn. Henna is, however, much better for your hair if you use it frequently.

As soon as you've turned your hair a convincing crimson hue, it's time to work on the rest of your ginger image. Get hold of some blue, green or hazel contact lenses and some pale foundation or white face paint. Then complete the look by applying freckles to your face with an orange marker pen.

Now start working on your redhead persona. Invent some stories about the gingerist abuse you received as a child. (The 'Ginger Insults' section should be able to provide you with some authentic terms.) Buy some high-factor suncream and nonchalantly leave it lying about. Find a photo of the Partridge Family, frame it, and put it on a wall at home.

Finally, if anyone tries to call your bluff about your hair colour, get really stroppy with them. They'll take this as a sign that you've got a fiery temper and proof that you're a genuine ginge. Simple.

RED CORNER

'It is observed that the red-haired of both sexes are more libidinous and mischievous than the rest, whom yet they much exceed in strength and activity.'

Gulliver's Travels,
Jonathan Swift

coming out of the ginger closet

It's time to pause and take a moment to reflect.

Perhaps you're flicking through this book in a shop. Perhaps you were bought it as a present. You may even be laughing at some of the gingas depicted throughout these pages. At the very least you will be sympathizing with their plight. But are you denying something that's glaringly obvious to everyone else? While you may think you've got 'strawberry blonde' or 'light brown' hair, are you in actual fact a ginga yourself? Consider:

We're here. We're ginger. Get over it!

- Have you found yourself buying suncream with a factor of over 30?
- Have you noticed that your entire body is covered in freckles?
- Have you found yourself craving Jaffa Cakes, ginger nuts or carrots?

If you answered 'yes' to at least two of the questions above, perhaps it's time for you to come out of the ginger closet.

The first thing you should accept is that being a ginge is nothing to be ashamed of. Gingerness isn't right or wrong – it's just the way you are.

The good news is that you're not alone. Glance down

The future's bright. The future's orange

your local high street and you'll see hundreds of fellow ginners, or thousands if you live in Scotland. Don't be afraid to express your solidarity with them, and ask for their advice about coping with the condition.

If you feel the time is right to confess your copper-topped nature, be careful. This isn't a perfect world, after all, and there is still much prejudice out there. You may find that your

ginger faq

Are gingers genetically superior?

As we've seen in the 'Hall of Fame' sections of this book, redheads have made an enormous contribution to the world despite being relatively few in number. But should we go as far as to conclude that gingers are just better than other people?

Maybe. But I think we would be getting into dangerous ginger-supremacist territory here. There is, after all, a simpler explanation for all this coppertopped overachievement.

Could it be that because gingers are unable to stay out in the sun as long as others, they're forced to go inside and pursue things that are more worthwhile than sunbathing and fannying about by the pool? It would explain a lot.

Ginger is beautiful

friends and family are perfectly relaxed about your hair colour. On the other hand, it may be that they never speak to you again – although such blatant intolerance is rare these days.

So, take heart. And don't feel that just because you've come out of the red-hair closet you automatically have to try and fit into the ginger scene. Sure, you may want to go to a ginger bar, drink Irn-Bru and party to Simply Red. That's absolutely fine. On the other hand you may not – gingerness is *your* lifestyle choice, and there's no correct or incorrect way to do it.

Actually, the top of a carrot is green, not orange

But whatever you chose to do, you'll certainly feel a lot better about yourself if you admit your true nature. So say it loud and say it proud – 'I'm ginger and I'm here to stay.'

I'm ginger and I'm here to stay

the ginger hall of fame:
ginger blasts from the past

Not all ginners achieve the lasting fame of Galileo, Shakespeare or
Churchill. Some enjoy their fifteen minutes and are never heard of again.
Below is a list of ginger bygones. Their stardom may have been fleeting,
but they still made a valuable contribution to the orange-haired community,
and one that's worth acknowledging.

Bingo – *The Banana Splits*
Strange ginger animal with dark glasses and buck teeth who played the
drums on Hanna-Barbera's hallucinogenic live-action show *The Banana
Splits*. Was probably intended to be some sort of monkey or gorilla.

The Partridge Family
Sitcom about a mostly ginger family who cope with the
loss of their father by driving about in a psychedelic
bus and performing pop songs.

Buzby
Indeterminable orange bird that featured on British
Telecom ads in the eighties, encouraging people to use

the phone. Voiced by Bernard Cribbins, Buzby's gentle approach contrasted sharply with the aggressive, Bob Hoskins-fronted emotional blackmail advertising campaign that followed.

Cabbage Patch Kid dolls
Dolls invented by American artist and toy manufacturer Xavier Roberts, with the gimmick that no two of them were exactly alike. Became a brief eighties craze, causing the traditional catfights for the last remaining stock on Christmas Eve. Many subtle variations upon the basic red-haired cabbage patch doll were released, which you could get a lot of money for on eBay if you were the kind of child who kept all your toys in their original packaging so they'd be worth more in the future. You freak.

Cuddles – *The Keith Harris Show*
Cheeky orange monkey and arch rival of Orville. Cuddles's catchphrase, 'I hate that duck!' struck a chord with nihilistic post-punk kids, but unfortunately the plastic primate never quite had the antiestablishment cred of rival puppet Spit the Dog.

Errol the Hamster – *The Roland Rat Show*
Ginger Welsh hamster who said, 'Roll VT' whenever he got into a comic scrape. Errol's been off our screens for a couple of decades now, but his memory has been kept alive by lookalike Brazilian footballer Ronaldo.

My Little Pony

Many of Hasbro's plastic ponies were ginger in some way, presumably so that young, carrot-topped girls would choose them. They included 'Bright Eyes', a blue pony with bright orange hair, 'Candy Kisses', a ginger pony with disturbing blue lipstick, and 'Jazzie', a red-haired pony who rather dangerously wore both roller skates and a Walkman.

Stuart 'Pogo' Patterson and Luke 'Gonch' Gardener

Funny how *Grange Hill*'s two most famous ginger characters were both employed to provide comic relief in their constant attempts to devise moneymaking schemes. Why didn't they get to do any of the 'issues' stuff like taking heroin or drowning in swimming pools?

Space Dust

Bright orange sherbet snack that fizzed in your mouth as you ate it. Apparently made your head explode if you combined it with a soft drink. No incidents of this occurring are officially recorded, but it did happen to a friend of a friend and that's the God's honest truth.

Space Hoppers

Rubbish seventies mode of transport. Space Hoppers were basically huge orange balloons with horns on top, and an evil smiley face printed on the front.

Although they were a brief children's fad, they failed to catch on as a serious mode of transport due to the fact that it took about ten times as long to get anywhere on a Space Hopper than it did on foot. They now live on as a nostalgic reference in stand-up comedy sets.

Strawberry Shortcake
A scented doll based on a red-haired Victorian street urchin. Surprisingly, the scent was strawberries rather than something more realistic like scabies.

Tails – *Sonic the Hedgehog*
A ginger fox with two tails who starred in Sega's Sonic games throughout the nineties. Although his extra tail allowed him to do lots of special spinning attacks, Tails never quite achieved Sonic the Hedgehog's level of fame and remained very much a ginger sidekick in the Ron Weasley and Art Garfunkel mode.

Tenderheart Bear
Tenderheart Bear was the ginger leader of the Care Bears, a group of effeminate bears who lived in the Kingdom of Caring and who encouraged children to share their feelings. Braveheart Lion, the leader of the spinoff Care Bear Cousins, was also a redhead, and came complete with a mane of hair that resembled a classic eighties ginger mullet.

how to make the world a gingerer place

If reading and learning about your hair heritage has inspired you to do more for the ginger cause, here are a few ways you can help. If everyone followed these few simple pointers, we'd all be able to enjoy a more carrot-friendly world.

Get a ginger pet

Ginger cats, red setters and goldfish are all popular choices for ginger fans. Just be careful not to be too unorthodox in your choice of ginger pet. Orang-utans, foxes and Highland cattle might make novelty house pets and provide a talking point at dinner parties, but don't be surprised if you get a few calls from the RSPCA. Especially if you keep them all in the same room.

Save the red squirrel

The UK's population of ginger squirrels is under threat from the fat grey ones, who are eating too much of the available food. So if you see a red squirrel, give them some nuts or build a special squirrel home for them. In a surprising pro-ginger move on the government's part, grey squirrels are classed as vermin, while the red ones are protected. Just as it should be.

Elect a ginger prime minister

Despite the efforts of Neil Kinnock, Paddy Ashdown and Charles Kennedy, Britain hasn't had a ginger PM since Churchill. And what's happened since then? The decline of British industry, the loss of our remaining Empire and humiliating defeat in several Eurovision song contests.

Demand equal rights

Write to the government and demand that they set up a Commissioner for Ginger Equality, which will address the rampant gingerism that's endemic in our society.

Boost ginger ratings

Turn on your telly whenever it's time for a show with a red-haired presenter such as Chris Evans or Anne Robinson. This will boost the ratings of ginger shows and encourage TV bosses to put more redheads on TV.

Remember that you only need to keep your TV turned on, though. I'm not suggesting that you actually watch *The Weakest Link*.

Support a ginger sidekick

For too long gingers have been in the shadows of their more famous friends. Address this by celebrating a redheaded sidekick. For example, head to your local bookshop and change the title of the first Harry Potter book to *Ron Weasley and Harry Potter and the Philosopher's Stone*.

Also consider buying an Art Garfunkel solo album, as well as writing to Danny Bonaduce and telling him that he was your favourite member of the Partridge Family, including David Cassidy.

Start a ginger religion

Devise a religion that acknowledges the sacred power of red hair. Gingers have a good track record here, as Scientology founder L. Ron Hubbard was one. However, his religion focused more on accessing past lives and agreeing fixed rates of donation than celebrating gingerness.

> ## RED CORNER
>
> 'When redheaded people are above a certain social grade their hair is auburn.'
>
> A Connecticut Yankee in King Arthur's Court, *Mark Twain*

the ginger hall of shame: scary gingers

The Ginger Survival Guide believes that gingerphobia is cruel and unnecessary. However, there are certain isolated cases where fear of gingers is justified. I mean, have you seen Anne Robinson's face recently?

Clowns

Nobody can quite remember who decided that garish ginger wigs, evil painted grins and creepy white face paint would constitute the costume of a character intended to entertain children. But the fact remains that you could hire Leatherface from *The Texas Chainsaw Massacre* to terrorize your children's party and it still wouldn't be as frightening as the average clown. Pennywise from *It* by Stephen King still provokes nightmares in grown men.

Anne Robinson

Ginger dominatrix who traumatizes contestants on *The Weakest Link* with her scripted put-downs and scary plastic face.

Thor

The Scandinavian god of thunder was traditionally depicted as a ginger who could fire lightning out of his ginger beard. Well, it would scare me.

Chuck Norris

Being, remarkably, a genuine ginger ninja, action-movie star Norris is so frightening he's even invented his own martial art called Chun Kuk Do, which incorporates kicking, striking and grappling. Even more frightening, though, is the fact that he's George W. Bush's favourite actor.

Satan

Gingerist hate crime throughout the ages has largely been justified by the belief that red hair is the mark of Satan, and that therefore all ginners are evil.

Banished from Heaven for waging a war against God, Satan now lives in Hell, where he divides his time between making mad people do things and recording backward messages for heavy-metal records.

Vampires

Given that they both have pale skin and fear sunlight, it's no surprise that the link between gingers and vampires has been made. However, since

Bram Stoker's *Dracula* fixed our idea of vampires as sexy dark-haired Eastern Europeans, the ginner variety has been far less common.

Chucky – *Child's Play* (and sequels)

Horror icon Chucky was a ginger-haired doll possessed by the spirit of a serial killer. On the plus side, this meant he could run on voodoo power rather than batteries. On the negative side, it meant that he killed everyone he came into contact with. So, overall, not a great Christmas gift.

Banshees

Mythical creatures with long ginger hair and pale skin who appear in front of you, screaming in your face, just before your death. If you think you've seen one, check that it's not just the local ginger goth before you get too worried.

Ginger – *Ginger Snaps*

In the cult Canadian horror movie *Ginger Snaps*, Ginger is a teenage girl who is bitten by a strange beast in the woods and gradually starts to transform into a werewolf. While this gives her more confidence with boys, it also means she develops a serious body-hair problem. Swings and roundabouts.

Leprechauns

Short, mythical creatures with ginger beards, hats and pipes. Like clowns, they aren't supposed to be scary, and even feature in a long-running US ad campaign for breakfast cereal Lucky Charms, where they delight children by coming to life and leaping off the box. But the fact remains that if one of these beings really did turn up in your kitchen one morning, your reaction would more likely be one of abject horror.

Witches

The belief that red hair was a mark of witchcraft was popular in the seventeenth century. These days, however, ginger witches don't get much scarier than the White Witch in *The Lion, The Witch And The Wardrobe*, and Willow from *Buffy The Vampire Slayer*.

a world without gingers

If you still don't believe that gingers have made an immeasurable contribution to world culture, take a glimpse into a nightmarish alternative universe where the Melanocortin-1 receptor gene never existed. Is this really the world you want to live in, gingerphobes?

We'd all be part of a German empire

Would the Allies have won the war without stern ginge Winston Churchill in charge of Britain? Maybe we'd all be eating sauerkraut, wearing lederhosen and listening to David Hasselhoff.

Starbucks would not exist

If ginger explorer Christopher Columbus hadn't chanced upon America, would the US as we know it exist? Without America we'd have no Americanization of the world. And without world Americanization we wouldn't have the skinny latte, the frappuccino or the caramel macchiato.

We wouldn't be able to say that something was 'excellent'

Shakespeare, who is shown undeniably ginge in some portraits, invented loads of the words he used, including 'excellent', 'obscene', 'pedant' and 'critical'. And Shakespeare wasn't the only redhead to enrich the English language. If it wasn't for ginge (bottle, admittedly) Geri Halliwell, the English language wouldn't have the word 'zigazagah'.

There'd be no Church of England

Following a spat with the Pope over his marital problems, randy ginge Henry VIII broke away from Rome and established an independent Church of England. So without him, we'd have no coffee mornings, no bric-a-brac sales and no Sir Cliff Richard.

Punk would never have happened

If it hadn't been for fake ginge Johnny Rotten and genuine ginge Malcolm McLaren, punk would never have replaced progressive rock, and we'd all still be listening to Rick Wakeman performing a three-hour mellotron solo on ice.

Science would be different

Ginger boffin Galileo Galilei has been called 'the father of science' for his part in the development of scientific method. And if we'd never had that we'd be living in a chilling dystopian world with no iPods or camera phones.

The world would be in peril

Without the tireless efforts of Daredevil, Chuck Norris and Daphne from *Scooby Doo*, the world would be under threat from villains such as Kingpin, Communist guerrilla groups and caretakers who dress up as ghosts to distract everyone from hidden treasure.

RED CORNER

'*Detective*: You Irish?
Miranda: No, why?
Detective: 'Cos you have beautiful red hair.
Miranda: Well, I guess anybody can be Irish with the right colourist.'
Sex and the City

138

the ginger hall of fame:
scottish gingers

With 13 per cent of the nation's population carrot-topped, red hair is as Scottish as shortbread, bagpipes and supporting whomever England are playing in the World Cup. But who are the red-locked Jocks who have defined Scotland as the spiritual home of ginners?

Billy Bremner

Diminutive footie hard man Bremner is fondly remembered by Scotland and Leeds United fans, as is his curly mop of ginger hair. By the time of his coaching career, however, the mop had diminished into the kind of threadbare comb-over that, by law, all eighties football managers were required to have.

Lord Byron

Famously described by his mistress Lady Caroline Lamb as 'Mad, bad and dangerous to know', Byron did little to dispel the fiery ginger stereotype. Unlike most of today's poets, he spent his free time shagging around and getting involved with wars, rather than teaching creative writing and appearing on late-night BBC Two discussion shows.

Robin Cook

The late Labour MP was renowned as a brilliant parliamentarian and debater. Unfortunately, his political career was held back by both his principled opposition to the war in Iraq and the fact that he looked like he should be sitting on a toadstool smoking a pipe.

Fat Bastard – *Austin Powers*

Unsurprisingly, the bagpipe-playing, kilt-wearing, baby-eating Scotch stereotype from the Austin Powers films was given a full head of red hair. And massive ginger sideburns, ginger back hair and downy ginger fluff on his bitch tits. Pleasant.

Charles Kennedy

When Kennedy took over the Liberal Democrats in 1997, ginger rule looked to be a possibility for Britain once again. Unfortunately, Kennedy was brought down by another stereotypical Scottish trait – being pissed out of his face.

Shirley Manson

There was a time when you'd have cowered in fear if you'd been confronted by a black-clad, pale-skinned ginner screaming at you (see 'Banshees', page 134). These days, however, rock fans pay good money for it.

Mary, Queen of Scots

Ginger monarch who was crowned Queen of Scotland when she was just nine months old. In 1587 she was executed by her cousin Elizabeth I, in a tragic early example of ginge-on-ginge violence.

Minnie the Minx

Eager to follow the success of Dennis the Menace, *The Beano* created ginger Scottish schoolgirl Minnie the Minx in 1953. Like a prototype Geri Halliwell, Minnie delivered redheaded girl power while looking much older than she was supposed to be.

Rob Roy

Ginger, kilt-wearing and hard as nails, Rob Roy could only have been more Scottish if he'd started taking heroin and listening to Runrig.

Jimmy Somerville

Ginger singer who had hits with Bronski Beat, The Communards and as a solo artist. Somerville was one of the few openly gay eighties stars, campaigning for gay rights and writing songs about homophobia back in the days when we all thought George Michael, The Pet Shop Boys and C-3PO were straight.

save the ginger: an appeal

As the sun rises on a bright spring morning, a door opens and a ginger emerges. Watch as it makes its way happily down the street, drinking Tizer and listening to T'Pau on its iPod.

But, believe it or not, this beautiful sight could soon be gone for ever. Some scientists predict that with the current pace of globalization and migration, the ginger gene could die out within the next hundred years.

Here at *The Ginger Survival Guide* we believe that ginners are creatures who deserve to live freely and happily in their natural habitat.

If you agree, please send as much as you can to our *Save the Ginger* appeal.

£10 ($18) will keep a family of five gingas in carrots for a month.
£5 ($9) will be enough to buy high-factor 50 suncream to prevent them from experiencing over-exposure and certain death.
And as little as £2.29 ($4) can buy a henna kit, so gingerness can live on after the gene has died out.
Please return this form with whatever donation you can afford.

Remember, this could be your last chance to make a difference to a coppertop.

Name

Address

Age

Donation

☐ Please tick this box if you do not wish to receive information about Jaffa Cakes or Orange Tango

the
ginger
survival guide

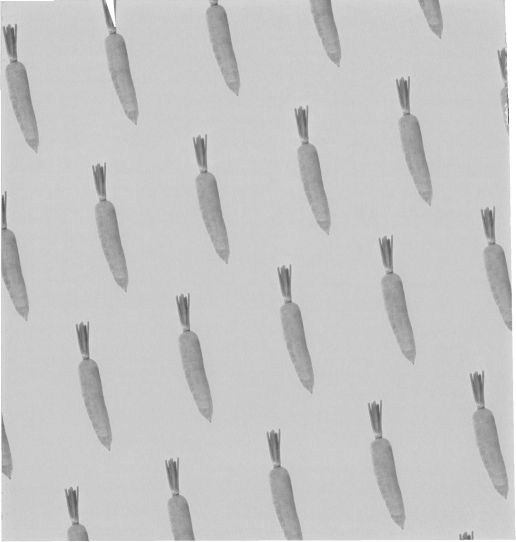